Rawls Explained

IDEAS EXPLAINED™

Daoism Explained, Hans-Georg Moeller

Frege Explained, Joan Weiner

Luhmann Explained, Hans-Georg Moeller

Heidegger Explained, Graham Harman

Atheism Explained, David Ramsay Steele

Sartre Explained, David Detmer

Ockham Explained, Rondo Keele

Rawls Explained, Paul Voice

IN PREPARATION

Phenomenology Explained, David Detmer

Deleuze and Guattari Explained, Rohit Dalvi

Rawls Explained

From Fairness to Utopia

PAUL VOICE

OPEN COURT
Chicago and La Salle, Illinois

Volume 8 in the Ideas Explained™ Series

To order books from Open Court, call toll-free 1-800-815-2280, or visit www.opencourtbooks.com.

Open Court Publishing Company is a division of Carus Publishing Company.

First printing 2011

Printed and bound in the United States of America.

Library of Congress Cataloging-in-Publication Data

Voice, Paul, 1958-
Rawls explained / Paul Voice.
p. cm. — (Ideas explained ; v. 8)
Includes bibliographical references and index.
ISBN 978-0-8126-9680-6 (trade paper : alk. paper) 1. Justice. 2. Rawls, John, 1921-2002. I. Title.
JC578.V65 2011
320.01'1—dc22

2010045983

The perspective of eternity is not a perspective from a certain place beyond the world of a transcendent being; rather it is a certain form of thought and feeling that rational persons can adopt within the world. And having done so, they can, whatever their generation, bring together into one scheme all individual perspectives and arrive together at regulative principles that can be affirmed by everyone as he lives by them, each from his own standpoint. Purity of heart, if one could attain it, would be to see clearly and act with grace and self-command from this point of view.

—JOHN RAWLS, *A Theory of Justice*

Contents

Acknowledgments

I would like to thank Sabine Merz for her help editing the text and Heather Kennon for constructing the index, as well as Bennington College for its generous leave policies that enabled me to write this book.

Introduction

John Rawls was the most important political philosopher of the twentieth century, although few people outside of the academic world are familiar either with his name or his ideas. At best, some will recall reading Rawls's work in their college classrooms. Part of the reason for this unearned obscurity is Rawls's reluctance to participate in public and political life. Another reason is that his work is not easily accessible either in content or style to readers unfamiliar with its intellectual context and its somewhat arcane vocabulary. However, barely a word of political philosophy is written today that is not indebted in some way, either directly or indirectly, to the philosophical paradigm that Rawls bequeathed. On his death at age eighty-one in 2002, his obituaries, written by some of the leading figures in Western philosophy, placed him alongside John Locke and Immanuel Kant in the canon of Western political philosophers. His colleague, the philosopher Hilary Putnam, said: "His work is not going to be forgotten for decades, I think, for centuries."

Rawls's life is not one to inspire a legion of biographers. He was born in 1921 in Baltimore, Maryland. After graduating from Princeton in 1943 he enlisted in the US Army and fought in Asia. He completed his graduate studies at Princeton and taught briefly at Oxford and various US universities before settling down to teach for most of his career at Harvard. He had a long and happy marriage and every account describes him as a generous, kind, and unassuming man. Putnam says that Rawls "didn't just think about how to do good and be good, but he seemed to exemplify in his own life doing good and being good."

The purpose of this short book is to introduce the reader to the political philosophy of Rawls. My aim is to explain the basic ideas of Rawls's theory of justice and to guide the reader through his arguments. I have divided the discussion into three parts corresponding to the three books that form the core of Rawls's theory: *A Theory of Justice* (1971), *Political Liberalism* (1993), and *The Law of Peoples* (1999). I set out Rawls's arguments in the form of a critical exposition and end each part with a survey of some of the main criticisms coupled with what I take to be Rawls's strongest counterarguments.

A Theory of Justice was first published in 1971. It is among the most important works of political philosophy of the twentieth century, some would argue the most important. Many of the main ideas Rawls sets out in the book were first published in a series of articles that stretched back to 1958. However, it is the vast ambition of the philosophical theory that Rawls offers in a single 500-plus-page text that captured the attention of the academy. *A Theory of Justice* is a sophisticated, deeply complex, and revolutionary theory of justice for democratic societies. It moves between discussions of morality to problems of rational choice, economic theory, and developmental psychology among many other topics. But it always keeps its focus on the central question: What are the principles that ought to govern the institutions of a just and stable democratic polity? It is the complexity of Rawls's thought and the systematic exposition of his arguments, coupled with his clarity of focus, that makes reading *A Theory of Justice* so rewarding. Furthermore, a careful reader cannot come away from time with this text without a sense that something very important has been said and also with the desire to engage critically with Rawls's arguments, the desire to wrestle with the ideas and to see how firmly they stand up to scrutiny. If we measure the importance of a book of philosophy by the number of other writers who use its ideas and who critically grapple with its arguments, then Rawls's *A Theory of Justice* stands very near the top of the scale.

Aside from the intrinsic merits of the work, *A Theory of Justice* was first published at a time when political philosophy was in need of a new perspective. The thought that one could take up the traditional question of justice, as it was asked by Aristotle or John Stuart Mill, was met with a general skepticism. To ask how societies *ought* to be governed so as to achieve justice was to court the ridicule of both positivists and Marxists. The former had reduced the scope of political philosophy to mere conceptual analysis; a method of making explicit how we use particular words. From the point of view of adjudicating the justice of particular institutions and societies, how people use the words they do was precisely what was in question and so beside the point. The Marxists renounced talk of justice as a particularly insidious form of ideological manipulation by the ruling class. For Marxists the issue was not ensuring that institutions are just and that the rights of citizens are secured but rather changing the material basis of society, ending class warfare, and making the very question of justice pointless.

On the other hand, libertarianism *was* a political philosophy that took the issue of justice and rights seriously. However, libertarians viewed the state and its institutions as obstacles to justice and viewed rights only as protections against state interference in the activities and projects of individuals. Moreover, libertarianism, by reducing the question of justice to noninterference and the elaboration of only negative rights, had little theoretical grasp of what were, to many, manifest injustices of material inequality and unequal opportunities and life prospects. Rawls's philosophy, as we will see, takes seriously the role of institutions in making social justice possible and it directly addresses inequalities of wealth, income, rights, and opportunities. Furthermore, rather than reconciling us to the "justice" of these inequalities Rawls advocates principles that would, if practically implemented, radically change the shape of society and the prospects of its citizens.

Thus, *A Theory of Justice* was published in an environment that was ready to renew the traditional questions of political philosophy and take seriously the issue of how the institutions of our society ought to be arranged to achieve justice. In many ways, political philosophy in the Anglo-American tradition since 1971 has been a footnote to *A Theory of Justice*, including Rawls's own later works. In the pages below I try to offer a clear but sufficiently nuanced explanation of the structure of Rawls's theory of justice as fairness. I offer as much complexity as I think is required for a firm grasp of the theory and that will provide the reader with a sufficiently good understanding of what Rawls is up to. I hope that this introduction to *A Theory of Justice* will encourage readers to take up the text itself and experience the excitement of philosophical discovery.

Rawls's second main text, *Political Liberalism*, was published twenty-two years after *A Theory of Justice* in a very different academic and political environment. Rawls had helped establish liberalism as the predominant political philosophy. Through the 1980s its main challenger was communitarianism, a view that challenged liberalism's commitment to individualism and its claims to universal justification. The main target of the communitarian critique was the position set forth in *A Theory of Justice.* Rawls presents *Political Liberalism* as a clarification of and an amendment to his earlier book. It collects and extends a set of arguments Rawls published in a number of articles through the 1980s. It contains a dazzling set of new concepts and ideas that transforms and challenges the traditional interpretation of what liberalism means. While *Political Liberalism* does not tackle the communitarian critique head-on, it shows how liberalism can answer the communitarian critique while maintaining liberalism's core ideas. In short, the aim of *Political Liberalism* is to demonstrate how justice is possible in a society in which citizens adhere to and advocate incompatible conceptions of the good. The problem of the plurality of conceptions of the good in democratic societies was not fully understood or addressed in *A Theory of Justice.* However, in confronting this problem Rawls makes clear that he intends the scope of the justification of his principles of justice to extend only to societies that have a history of democratic institutions and to persons who share a conception of the good that includes a particular understanding of the nature of persons as free and equal.

Therefore, in addressing the problem of pluralism in democratic societies Rawls distinguishes his version of liberalism from theories of liberalism that claim an ahistorical, universal justification of their principles of justice. Advocates of this latter form of liberalism often called on *A Theory of Justice* in support of their arguments and proposed a clear distinction between Rawls's earlier and later work, claiming that Rawls's views have changed. As I have said, Rawls himself is very clear that *A Theory of Justice* and *Political Liberalism* are theoretically continuous, a point he makes abundantly clear in the final book, *Justice as Fairness.* My approach is to treat Rawls's work as a single theory and to read *A Theory of Justice* in light of the ideas and arguments in *Political Liberalism.* This approach greatly enriches and clarifies the ideas in the former text.

The third and final book that the present work examines is *The Law of Peoples*, published in 1999. It is based on ideas Rawls developed in a lecture and short article in the early 1990s. While Rawls's previous work was devoted to the problem of justice within democratic societies *The Law of Peoples* examines the problem of international justice. His approach to the issue is provocative and deeply controversial among liberal political thinkers. Taking the value of toleration as foundational he declines the temptation to argue for the application of the principles of justice he advocates for liberal democratic polities to all societies. He goes on to make a number of important distinctions between, for example, nation-states and peoples, and between liberal and decent societies. Given the general preoccupation with the problems of globalization Rawls's contribution stands at the center of the debate, even if it receives a great deal of criticism, and, in my opinion, is often misunderstood.

I first came across *A Theory of Justice* as an undergraduate in an ethics class. What made such an enormous impact on me was the way Rawls provided the vocabulary and theoretical tools to carve out a space between value relativism and a metaphysical realism about values. I felt I could, at last, say something substantive about justice using Rawls's ideas that was not merely a reflection of my background and interests, but also did not entail a commitment to either a deity or a metaphysically dubious realm of moral reality. I found many of Rawls's arguments difficult, abstract, and complex. However, they were also presented in a ruthlessly systematic fashion and often with admirable elegance. Reading Rawls I was introduced to an entirely new way of thinking about the possibilities of philosophy. I have seen this reaction many times in my own students and I hope to convey in this book something of the sense of wonder I experienced on first reading Rawls. Another aspect of Rawls's work that I hope to convey to the reader is his ability to connect the abstract world of philosophical argument with immediate and practical concerns. Rawls is always alert to the historical place of his ideas and their implications for how societies are organized and the way people live their lives. Underlying the steel-like arguments is an abundantly evident interest in changing the world and a belief in the possibility of making a difference.

My aim, as the title of this book announces, is to explain Rawls's ideas. I say nothing more here about Rawls's life and I do not engage in the more arcane debates that interest only a few scholars. For readers who wish to follow up on a line of argument, I provide a selected bibliography at the end of each of the three parts of the book.

Part One
A Theory of Justice

It is a challenge to plunge straight into *A Theory of Justice*; many readers are unfamiliar with a normative approach to questions of justice and also unfamiliar with the place of Rawls's text in the history of political philosophy. Therefore, before we engage with the theory directly, I want to present two introductory ideas that provide a context and direction to our task of understanding the complexities and challenges of *A Theory of Justice*. The first is the idea of reasonable hope and the second the idea of imaginative identification.

1. Two Introductory Ideas

The Idea of Reasonable Hope

A philosophical theory of justice is *normative*; it argues for how things *should* be rather than stating how matters, in fact, stand. A political philosopher does not set out to discover what people think justice *is*; she instead says what people *ought* to think about justice. To many readers this will seem, at first, too disengaged from the concrete problems of actual societies and the injustices suffered by real people; utopian thought is for the armchair, whereas what is required, they might think, is the practicality of action. However, this stark dichotomy of what is the case and what ought to be the case is deeply misleading and the first step to grasping the power of Rawls's theory of justice is to avoid it. First, any plausible theory of justice, while being normative, has to be anchored in the realities of human nature and the possibilities of human society; if we ought to be angels then a theory of justice will be of interest only to angels. Second, any plausible theory of justice must challenge and extend our sense of moral and political agency. A theory of justice challenges us to go beyond ourselves and reach towards what we are not yet but what we might become. This requires an act of imagination: the projection of ourselves into an imagined and possible future. A plausible theory of justice then navigates the line between extravagant utopianism and the hopelessness of despair.

In *The Critique of Practical Reason*, the German Enlightenment philosopher Immanuel Kant said there were three great questions in philosophy: What can I know? What ought I to do? and What can I hope for? While the first two questions are at the forefront of Rawls's political philosophy, the idea of hope is also a constant background theme. Rawls makes the idea of hope explicit for the first time late in his career when he tackles the problem of international justice. He uses two phrases to describe the line he follows in his account of how international justice is possible: the line between an unanchored utopianism and a hopeless realism. The first is the idea of a "realistic utopia" and the second is the idea of "reasonable hope."

The former phrase brings together the two parts of the dichotomy and invites us to consider Rawls's philosophy as a fusing of a concern with the real and a concern with the utopian. Rawls's account of international justice has received criticism from skeptics who think its demands are too limited and from others who think it demands too much. The idea of a realistic utopia is useful since it designates the middle path Rawls treads between these critical positions. Hope is an attitude of positive expectation. We do not hope for what we will certainly receive nor do we hope for what we acknowledge is impossible. Hope takes us, in a leap of imagination, from what is to what might be. A philosophical theory of justice, insofar as it is normative, thus relies on the attitude of hope in the reader for its persuasiveness by asking us to answer the question: Is the realization of the world according to this theory worth hoping for? As we assemble and connect the parts of Rawls's theory we should keep this question in mind. We should also keep in mind that hope is connected to action. A sincere hope for some state of affairs motivates an agent to act to bring it about if possible and, on balance, desirable. In this way, Rawls's theory of justice is *political* in the sense of being a practical vision of a possible better world.

Finally, we should consider the idea of *reasonable* hope. The "reasonable" in the phrase "reasonable hope" encompasses two dimensions. First, it stands between the vain hope of the fanatic who reaches for an impossible world and the absence of hope that pervades the mind of the skeptic. Thus, a reasonable person hopes for what is possible and values the possibilities of the future. There is, however, another sense of "reasonable," one that is particular to Rawls's philosophy and which we will come across many times in the pages that follow. This is the idea that a reasonable person is one who proposes principles and courses of action that others have reason to accept (or not reject). Therefore, in the context of a theory of justice, reasonable hope is a desire for a future world that others in one's own society or in other societies, could, in principle, accept. This is also another way hope is rendered political, namely, by making it a social attitude that engages with the lives of others.

Rawls's writing is not evangelical; he rarely prods his readers' consciences directly. He uses the language of the professional philosopher, somewhat dry and sometimes quite technical. However, a full appreciation of the power of his work requires that we keep the idea of reasonable hope before us because it is this powerful political attitude that is the oxygen that sustains and makes vivid the theory as a whole.

The Idea of Imaginative Identification

Rawls's approach to answering the questions of justice is *contractarian*. He follows in the tradition of the great contract theorists, such as Thomas Hobbes (1588–1679), John Locke (1632–1704), and Jean-Jacques Rousseau (1712–1778). These philosophers were concerned with answering the following question: Why should people obey the laws of the state? In other words, they asked: What are the grounds for the state's authority? They provided quite different answers to this important question but they shared a common method of answering it. Hobbes, for example, considers a world without any government, what he called a "state of nature." What, he asks, would motivate people in a state of nature to give up their natural liberties and agree to submit to the authority of the state? In Hobbes's case the answer turns out to be obvious. The state of nature is such an awful place that only an authoritarian government would guarantee citizens' against falling back into a "war of all against all." What motivates Hobbes's people is a very sharp sense of their own interests: they are rational egoists. Thus, they would agree, as rational agents, to forego the anarchic freedoms of the state of nature and submit to the authority of the state. Locke offers a much more benign description of the state of nature and his contractors enter into civil society for its "conveniences." More specifically, they need institutions to settle disputes, secure property, and provide security. However, the basic structure of a contract theory is evident here as well: submission to authority is an advantage that the contractors recognize and therefore agree to.

There are a number of background premises in Hobbes's and Locke's philosophies that we need to make plain to fully grasp the contractarian's approach to answering philosophical questions. We can get to them by asking why we, the readers, should care what fanciful agreements Hobbes's or Locke's contractors make? We care because contract theorists make claims about human nature and go on to argue that since we, the readers, share in that nature, we too would agree to the same contract. Thus, if it is rational for Hobbes's contractors to enter into an agreement submitting to the authority of the state, then it would be likewise rational for us to do so as well, so long as we share, in a fundamental way, the basic nature and motivations of Hobbes's contractors. However, we need more than this for a satisfying explanation. First, we need to add that we would choose as they do, provided we are in relevantly similar circumstances. Therefore, we have to agree that the circumstances the contractors find themselves in are possible ones for us. Second, not only do the contractors have our motivations and share our possible circumstances, but also they reason in the way we would reason. Based on these four premises we can now see much more clearly how an agreement that we are not personally a party to can engage our interest and demand our philosophical consent. In short, we are called on to imaginatively identify with the contractors and reason along with them and, if everything is in place, we will have just as much reason to agree to the principles they choose as they do.

There are two further consequences of the contract theory approach. First, the claim is not merely that we, the readers, will agree along with the contractors, but that the fact of agreement constitutes a *justification* of the terms of agreement. Locke, for example, connects agreement with justification by way of the idea of consent. For Locke, in agreeing to submit to the (limited) authority of the state, this authority is justified by our consent. We should be cautious here to ensure that such consent is genuine and free, but setting these worries aside, we should notice the *normative* character that agreements have for contract theorists. For them the principles we (genuinely) agree to are the principles that we ought to abide by. Second, contract theorists suppose that our agreements are sources of *motivation*. For example, not only do we agree to the authority of the state, but also it is the fact of this agreement that motivates us to abide by its laws.

We have noted six background premises to the contract approach as it was traditionally understood. We can call this *the argument for imaginative identification*. These premises are:

1. The contractors and readers have a shared nature.
2. What the contractors agree to, we the readers would also agree to.
3. The contractors' circumstances are possible for us.
4. The contractors reason as we would.
5. Genuine agreements are normative; their content offers a justification.
6. Genuine agreements are motivating.

Although Rawls is a contractarian, his brand of contract theory is very different from the tradition he draws on, as we will see below. However, he shares with his predecessors the general approach of the argument for imaginative identification. Let us now consider the ways in which Rawls *differs* from the contract tradition.

In *A Theory of Justice* (TJ) Rawls says that his "aim is to present a conception of justice which generalizes and carries to a higher level of abstraction the familiar theory of the social contract" (TJ: 10). First, the "familiar" theories of Hobbes, Locke, and Rousseau all describe a possible place and time in which people lived in a state of nature (we should not read this to mean that they thought that such a time and place actually existed). They describe in some detail the possible circumstances in the state of nature. We are asked, in other words, to imagine an empirically realizable situation. Rawls abstracts from possible time and place and also from realizability. We are asked instead to imagine an "initial situation" that corresponds with a state of nature but which contains only the most abstract features. We, the empirically real readers, could have been in a Hobbesian state of nature, but, as we will see, we could not literally enter the initial situation that Rawls has in mind. The initial situation (Rawls's version of which he calls the "original position") is a thought experiment that abstracts from the empirical world we inhabit.

Second, the purpose of Rawls's agreement is not the justification of the exercise of political authority, but rather the justification of principles of political and distributive justice. Thus, Rawls's contract theory has both a different imaginative character and a different purpose. The situation in which the contractors come to agreement is a thought experiment and the object of their agreement is principles of justice. The abstraction clears away the messiness of a fantasy history which invites irrelevant questions. What matters for Rawls is only what is needed to characterize the contractors and their motivations, along with their circumstances and reasoning. He has no need for the lurid details of Hobbes's state of nature or the arguably more appealing details of Rousseau's alternative version. The change of the purpose of agreement to agreement on principles of justice considerably widens the scope of Rawls's argument. It extends beyond the question of legitimacy of the state to the fundamentals of the rules governing the basic institutions of our society. This is the nature of the invitation that Rawls extends to his readers: an invitation to imaginative identification with contractors in an abstract initial situation searching for agreement on principles of justice.

Rawls calls his account of justice "*justice as fairness.*" The basic idea of justice as fairness is simple. He argues that people in a situation that is fair will agree to principles that are themselves fair and that define what justice is for their society. This basic idea hides many philosophical assumptions. We will bring these assumptions to the surface and critically examine them. As we move through the arguments we should keep in mind the idea of reasonable hope as a guide to the purpose of Rawls's theory and read his account both as critical outsiders and with what I have called an imaginative identification with the contractors.

The following discussion is divided into three main sections. In the first, "The Analytic of Justice," I explain the main ideas of the theory and detail how Rawls's principles of justice are derived. The second section is "The Practicum of Justice" in which we examine how Rawls understands the practical application of his principles to constitutional, legislative, and administrative matters. In the final section of part one, I investigate the theoretical basis of Rawls's argument. I explore the type of justification Rawls employs in his argument for his justice principles and his discussion of the intersection of the right and the good. Finally, at the end of the section, I consider the problem of the stability of a just society.

2. The Analytic of Justice

The Original Position

The version of the initial situation that contractarians have traditionally called "states of nature" Rawls calls the "original position." Our first task in the analytic of justice is to assemble and connect the various elements that Rawls includes in the original position. This will enable us to understand how he derives and justifies his two principles of justice from the original position.

Contract theories have a common structure and Rawls's theory shares this structure. Below is a diagram of the basic contractarian structure and the elements that combine to form a full theoretical exposition of a contractarian theory of political obligation or justice. Any contractarian theory has to give an account of persons, their circumstances, their method of reasoning, the objects of their deliberation, and, finally, the principles that govern society. These elements are part of a dynamic process that moves from an initial situation through an act of agreement to civil society. It is useful to emphasize the dynamic character of contract theories, Rawls's included. They have the form of a narrative in which the concern that moves the plot along is the question of what principles the persons in the original position will finally subscribe to. Our aim is to move through this narrative of philosophical discovery and arrive at a satisfying and plausible outcome.

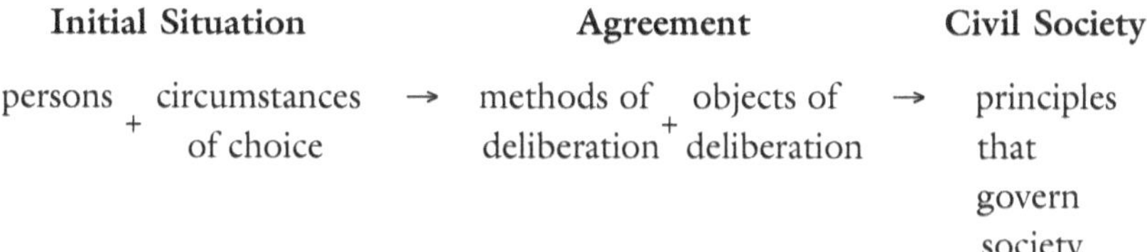

For example, Hobbes's contract theory of political obligation describes the initial situation as a state of nature, persons as rational egoists, and their circumstances as a "war of all against all." Their method of deliberation is a *modus vivendi* bargain, the object of their deliberations is to determine the extent of the powers of a sovereign to whom they surrender their "natural liberties," and finally the contractors arrive at a principle of absolute sovereign authority (with some provisos). Thus, once we have filled in the account a philosopher has given of each of these elements, or moments, we will have a clear view of their theory as a whole. In the following sections we will follow this diagram and explain each of the elements in Rawls's theory. This approach will enable us to understand Rawls's ideas while keeping in mind their place in the overall theory.

PERSONS

Who are Rawls's contractors? Earlier we noted that the argument for imaginative identification required that we share a "nature" with the contractors. Rawls has a different interpretation of this step in the argument from the classical contractarian theorists. Instead of arguing that the properties he assigns to the contractors constitute their (and our) "nature" (*what* we are essentially and universally) he claims that we share a "self-understanding" with the contractors who represent our "self-understanding" in the original position. What does this mean? Rawls claims that he is offering an argument for principles of justice that apply to a particular, historically determinate, society. By this he means a society that has a history and tradition of democratic institutions. He is not claiming to have answered the Socratic question "What *is* justice?" In short, the scope of the principles he offers is limited to liberal democratic societies. He offers his contractors as examples of how we, the citizens of a liberal democratic state, understand ourselves in our essential characteristics. Rawls narrows the scope of his aims in contrast to the traditional contract view because he believes judgments about the universal nature of persons are fundamentally controversial. These kinds of judgments are "metaphysical" and thus always open to dispute. However, he believes that we can nonetheless identify characteristics that constitute a shared, public, understanding of who we are as citizens of a democratic society. The contrast here between the "nature of persons" and "the shared understanding of citizens" was not made clear in *A Theory of Justice*, as Rawls himself acknowledges. So what are the characteristics that form the shared understanding of democratic citizens? Rawls identifies four main candidates: persons are rational, reasonable, free, and equal. We will examine each of these characteristics separately and see how the contractors exemplify them as aspects of what Rawls calls their "moral personality."

Moral Personality

Persons as Rational

Rawls's contractors are rational. A person is rational if she minimally meets the following three conditions: she is capable of having an end or purpose, her ends and purposes matter to her, and she is capable of arranging the means at her disposal to bring about her ends and achieve her purposes. In Rawls's language a person who meets these three criteria has a "conception of the good." What a person freely seeks to bring about (from a particular action such as a simple brush stroke to a complex state of affairs like world peace) is part of her idea of the good. Her life goes well insofar as she brings about the realization of her good (or if it is brought about by others) and goes badly if it is not. This takes care of having ends and these ends mattering to a person. What links the ends and caring for these ends is the ability and desire to intervene in the world as an efficient actor. The notion of efficiency refers to a capacity to manipulate elements of the world through actions and decisions that lead to the effective realization of the ends desired.

Rawls's contractors are rational, then, in the sense explained above. A note of caution should be added at this stage. It is tempting to think that all rational agents are self-interested agents. It is true that self-interested people can be rational but not all rational people are self-interested. This is important to keep in mind when reading Rawls. Rawls's contractors, unlike Hobbes's, are not egoists. A person who devotes her life to charity work has an end that matters to her and she may be efficient and effective in the realization of her charity work. Therefore, although she is altruistic she is nonetheless rational.

In the original position Rawls's contractors will make rational choices between candidate principles of justice. This is to say that they will seek to advance the realization of their conception of the good when making this choice. However, as we will see when we discuss the circumstances in which they make their choices, the contractors will know only *that* they have a conception of the good, not what it is. This will force them to make choices that will advance (or not damage) their conception of the good *whatever* it turns out to be.

Persons as Reasonable

In the original position Rawls's contractors know that they are reasonable and that their fellow contractors are reasonable. Reasonableness here has a narrow definition. A reasonable person is one who is capable of "entering into and abiding by fair terms of agreement." The contractors are therefore able to understand the terms of an agreement they make, act in accord with an agreement, and apply the principles in appropriate situations. There are two provisos here. First, the contractors undertake to abide by agreements once they "enter" civil society only providing others also abide by them (for the most part). Second, the contractors undertake to abide by agreements that are fair. These provisos are important because it would be irrational to abide by an agreement if other parties defect from it, and it would be unreasonable to abide by agreements that are unfair; it is unreasonable to abide by agreements that someone else has good reason to reject.

In the original position the contractors are reasonable in this minimal sense; they have the relevant capacities. In the original position this minimal understanding of reasonableness is described by Rawls as a "sense of justice." Rawls actually has a larger sense of the idea of reasonableness that we will examine later when we look at the requirements of democratic citizenship. These requirements include a willingness to offer "public reasons" in political communication and a willingness to accept the "burdens of judgment" when considering competing political claims. For now though, we should understand that Rawls's contractors are reasonable insofar as they have a sense of justice.

Self-Conception

Persons as Free

The idea that people are free is central to a democratic and liberal world view. We should distinguish between three quite different senses in which one might be free. First, there is a metaphysical sense of freedom. This implies that people's actions, beliefs, and intentions are not wholly determined by the past. They can escape the deterministic causal network. We might say people choose freely. When Rawls asserts that persons are free he is not committed to this controversial metaphysical doctrine. Second, there is a moral sense of freedom. People who are free in the moral sense are thereby responsible for their actions (and possibly their beliefs and intentions). Rawls does not deny this, but the extent of a person's moral responsibility depends on his particular moral beliefs and thus, on the particular conception of the good he embraces. Rawls does not understand a person's freedom in this moral sense nor in a metaphysical sense. Rather, he understands freedom in a third, political, sense. Persons can be free only within a society with appropriate institutions (yet to be defined) among others who are also free. Citizens' freedom is expressed in three capacities. First, they have a conception of the good that they are capable of revising and changing. Second, they have the capacity to make demands on social institutions to advance their conception of the good ("they regard themselves as sources of self-authenticating claims" [TJ: 32]). Third, they have the capacity to adjust their ends in the light of what it is reasonable to expect against a background of just institutions. Now these capacities for freedom are the ground for the claim that the contractors and citizens in a democratic society are autonomous. Persons are free for Rawls if they are *autonomous*.

People can be autonomous in two ways: they can be rationally autonomous and they can be fully autonomous. To be rationally autonomous is to be rational and reasonable according to the narrow definition set out earlier (to have a conception of the good and a sense of justice). In the original position the contractors are rationally autonomous. However, in a well-ordered democratic society citizens can attain full autonomy, by which Rawls means that they can organize their lives by acting in accord with freely chosen principles. This latter understanding of autonomy is only possible for citizens in a democratic society. So when we think of the contractors in the original position we should think of them as exhibiting a distilled understanding of persons as free. Therefore, our question will be: "What would rationally autonomous persons agree to as the principles to govern the basic institutions of society?" The answer to this question tells us what principles would be freely chosen by democratic citizens in a well-ordered society in which they can exercise their freedom to the fullest extent, in which they are fully autonomous.

Persons as Equal

Equality is another central democratic and liberal ideal. However, it is difficult to specify in what in sense people are supposed to be equal. For Rawls we once again need to differentiate equality between citizens and equality between the contractors in the original position. Contractors are situated in the original so that certain differences between them are elided. More specifically, they are denied knowledge about their own interests and powers and place in society. I will say much more about this later when we discuss the circumstances of the contractors. The contractors are equal with respect to one another insofar as they are equally situated. Knowledge of possible inequalities of knowledge, talent, powers, and capacities are denied to them.

Citizens are equal in a different way. Equality between citizens is the result of just basic institutions and is only achievable through institutional means. The idea of equality for Rawls only makes sense in the context of some institutional framework. Rawls insists on political equality (equality of political rights) but allows for inequalities in welfare (within a fairly narrow margin) and inequalities in life outcomes. This means that in a constitutional democracy equality of rights is guaranteed, but inequalities in how well citizens do in their lives are permitted, provided these inequalities result from the operation of just institutions. For Rawls, people are equal in the fundamental sense that they have equal political standing with respect to fellow citizens and equal claims on society's institutions.

The claim before us is that as citizens of a society with a tradition of democratic institutions we understand ourselves to be rational, reasonable, free, and equal. The original position distills this self-understanding and asks what rational and reasonable contractors, who are free in the sense of being rationally autonomous and who are situated equally with respect to one another would choose as the principles to govern the basic institutions of their society.

CIRCUMSTANCES OF CHOICE

Before we can follow the reasoning of the contractors in the original position we need to know the circumstances in which they make their choices between candidate principles of justice. These circumstances comprise both their situation and the constraints imposed on them. They are in the "circumstances of justice" and they face epistemic and motivational constraints.

Circumstances of Justice

The contractors are in the circumstances of justice. The question of justice itself only arises in the presence of these circumstances and so we should not be surprised that the contractors face them. The contractors would lack an incentive to reach an agreement on principles of justice if the circumstances described below did not prevail. In fact, there would be no reason to agree to anything since the question of the distribution of rights and resources would not occur to them.

Objective Circumstances

The objective circumstance of justice is the fact of moderate scarcity. The basic resources available to persons in any human society in which the question of justice arises are scarce. It is because of this scarcity that the question of the *distribution* of resources between citizens arises. If we imagine a society in which there is an abundance of resources, where every need and want can easily be met, then we would not trouble ourselves to allocate bundles of resources to particular people. We do not regulate the distribution of air for breathing because there is an abundance of it. We do regulate the distribution of gasoline (through prices) and the distribution of vaccine (through need) because gas and vaccines are scarce.

The scarcity of resources we are talking about here is what Rawls calls a *moderate* scarcity. This means that there must be enough of a particular resource to make the question of its distribution a problem with a possible solution. If, for example, there was so little food that almost no one's needs could be met, there would be no point in conjuring up a principle for its distribution. So, the question of justice arises when we find ourselves in a situation where the availability of resources is somewhere between abundance and absolute scarcity. This is our usual situation with respect to the goods most important to our lives as citizens and this situation is reflected in the original position. The contractors understand that the objective circumstances of justice apply to the society for which they are choosing principles.

SUBJECTIVE CIRCUMSTANCES

Not only do the citizens face a moderate scarcity of resources they also confront a conflict of interests with other citizens. Not all interests of all citizens can be met and satisfied. Citizens have different conceptions of the good and realizing these conceptions and acquiring the resources to achieve their conception of the good brings them into conflict with other citizens who seek their, perhaps quite different, conception of the good. Even people who share a conception of the good will often differ about how best to realize it. The basic point is that given our individual, subjective sets of interests, we will find ourselves in conflict with others whose interests differ. This will be true even if there is an abundance of external resources. For example, my interest in the world being arranged in a particular way, for instance, according to some religious doctrine, will conflict with your interest in a different world arrangement. No amount of resources will make this conflict disappear. We might say that the subjective circumstances of justice make us seek an arrangement that maximally allows us to pursue our interests and thus we seek a distribution not of resources as such, but of liberties and opportunities. Naturally these liberties and opportunities usually require external resources, but a just society attends to fundamental conflicts of interests as well as the distribution of external resources. The contractors are, of course, aware of the subjective circumstances of justice when considering what principles to choose.

Epistemic Constraints

We should remind ourselves at this point that Rawls's theory of justice is justice as *fairness*. We already discussed the purpose of the original position is to lay out a situation in which the contractors are forced to choose in circumstances that are fair. We need to emphasize that the contractors do not themselves act from motives of fairness; they do not seek to be fair in their dealing with their fellow bargainers. Instead they aim at advancing their own conception of the good whatever that turns out to be. Of course, acting fairly *may* turn out to be one of their fundamental values, but they do not know this.

So the question here is how do we make the original position fair if the contractors themselves are not motivated by fairness? One of Rawls's most striking innovations is the idea of a "veil of ignorance." This veil prevents the contractors knowing particulars about themselves that would unfairly advantage them in arriving at an agreement on principles of justice.

The Veil of Ignorance

The veil of ignorance prevents the contractors from knowing the following facts about themselves:

> First of all, no one knows his place in society, his class position or social status; nor does he know his fortune in the distribution of natural assets and abilities, his intelligence and strength and the like. Nor, again, does anyone know his conception of the good, the particulars of his rational plan of life, or even the special features of his psychology such as his aversion to risk or liability to optimism or pessimism. More than this, I assume that the parties do not know the particular circumstances of their society. That is, they do not know its economic or political situation, or the level of civilization and culture it's been able to achieve. The persons in the original position have no information to which generation they belong. (TJ: 118)

The range of facts here is very wide and we should categorize them. There are (a) facts about their own *nature* they do not know. They are ignorant of their "natural assets and abilities," and particular aspects of their psychology such as their attitude to risk. They are also (b) ignorant of their *place* in society. They do not know (c) what they *value* (only that they do value something). They are (d) ignorant of how their own *society* fares economically and politically. Lastly, (e) they have no idea to which *generation* they belong. In short, the veil of ignorance prevents the contractors from knowing their nature, their place, their particular values, particular facts about their society, and their generation.

Before we discuss each of these concealed facts in detail we should make the general point that Rawls considers that knowledge of these facts will make the situation between the contractors unfair. Further that the resulting principles agreed on in the original position would likewise be unfair and therefore unjust. What is concealed behind the veil of ignorance therefore offers us an important clue to what Rawls means by fairness. It is not that knowing one's nature *makes* people choose unfairly, but that, in Locke's words, we are "poor judges in our own cases." There is a certain moral frailty that we suffer as humans that is likely to prevent us from rising above our own circumstances and viewing a problem from a point of view that does not privilege ourselves.

We should keep in mind that we might agree that a veil of ignorance is required to ensure fairness in the original position (and therefore justice), but still disagree with Rawls about what facts should be placed behind the veil. As so often with Rawls, we need to keep the structure of his account separate from its details to ensure that we do not muddle a criticism of a detail with a rejection of the theory as a whole. I will now discuss each limitation on knowledge in more detail.

1. *Nature.* This is one of the most controversial limitations on knowledge that Rawls insists on. The contractors know that people have talents, aptitudes, and orientations that seem to have been delivered to them by nature. A talent for music or mathematics is an obvious example. A willingness to work hard, an aptitude for leadership, bodily strength, superior hand-eye coordination, physical attractiveness, being articulate, and so on are all assets that may be grounded in our nature. Why should the contractors be denied this information? This is an especially pressing question since my natural assets belong to me in an obvious way; after all, who else *could* they belong to? I want to look at two responses to this challenge. First, although these talents are indeed ours we have done nothing to deserve them. Natural assets are, in their very nature, gifts not rewards. As Rawls says, these gifts come to us via the "lottery of birth." They belong to us in the sense of finding ourselves in possession of them (like a person's red hair "belongs" to her), not in the sense of there being a wage for work done. The second response is to point out that a natural aptitude is not an asset unless a society rewards aptitudes of that kind. In a society that extravagantly rewards superior hand-eye coordination (chiefly among males) then an aptitude that allows one to effectively swing a baseball bat becomes a considerable asset. The same sort of consideration applies to all the other natural assets as well (think of different standards of beauty in different societies at different times). These two responses combined allow us to argue that natural assets are unearned advantages that are contingent on social arrangements. Since they are

unearned and contingent it would be unfair to allow contractors who possess these talents to tailor principles of justice to reward their own particular aptitudes. It is important to avoid a common misunderstanding of Rawls's position at this point. Rawls is not arguing that someone else, or the state, owns our natural assets. He is only arguing that, as far as justice is concerned, it is an open question who is to *benefit*, and by how much, from the exercise of natural aptitudes. When we remember that the contractors seek their own good in the original position we see also (a) that in denying them knowledge of their natural assets Rawls makes the question of rewards open and (b) that this ensures fairness in their deliberations. Many readers will still be uneasy about this move in the argument and I will return to the issue when I consider criticisms at the end of part one.

2. *Place.* This limitation on knowledge is easier to defend. Contractors who know their class position or status in society would, of course, seek to advantage their class and thereby advantage themselves. Class membership entails an ideology that is difficult to resist. What someone takes to be best for society may simply reflect the ideology of their class. In other words, our conceptions of the good are most often not unconnected to the ideology that supports the class structure of society. Members of advantaged classes often take their disproportionate share of society's benefits to be a reward for their hard work and remain blind to the advantages the lottery of birth has conferred on them. The class status of the family in which one is born is the surest indicator of success in life. We do not, after all, deserve our parents, rich or poor. Only an aristocratic conception of justice would suppose that we deserve our place in society simply in virtue of the time and place of our birth.

3. *Values.* If the contractors know what they value, what their conception of the good is, then they will shape the principles of justice to advance their own values. However, since we already know that the contractors operate under the assumption that the circumstances of justice prevail and that citizens' interests and values are diverse, we also know that there is significant disagreement about what constitutes the

good in society. The question is how we are to respect this diversity of values in the original position. One way is to design principles of justice that do not unfairly favor one or another particular conception of the good. This is achieved by denying the contractors information about their values. They must choose principles not knowing what their values are. Thus they are forced to respect all values (for this is the only way they can get respect for their own).

4. *Society.* The contractors choose principles for any society that treasures freedom, equality, and autonomy. The range of possible societies that meet this criterion is potentially broad. Different constitutional arrangements are possible and different levels of wealth and welfare are likewise possible. Such societies may prosper in different climates among peoples with culturally diverse attitudes and beliefs. Too much information about the details of a particular society would skew the deliberations of the contractors towards considering the fortunes of only one type of possible democratic society. The contractors therefore are ignorant of the details of their society and choose principles for democratic societies as a class rather than for a particular token democratic society.

5. *Generation.* Finally, the contractors do not know to which generation they belong. This forces them to consider questions of justice *between* generations. Rational agents, seeking their own good, might externalize costs associated with their own benefits and advantages onto future generations. An obvious example is environmental damage cause by fossil fuel energy that impacts future persons who bear the costs of the energy but do not enjoy the benefits. Furthermore, contractors have to consider reserving some of society's capital for later use. How much this should be is the subject of a "just savings principle" that should be part of the overall conception of justice for a democratic society.

These then are the facts that are concealed from the contractors by the veil of ignorance. We should remind ourselves that the contractors do know general facts about societies (they have basic economic and sociological knowledge), they know general facts about how people behave and think (they have basic psychological knowledge), and they have a conception of the good (they just don't know what it is).

In summary, Rawls is asking us to consider what rational and reasonable contractors would agree to in the original position where they are situated so they are ignorant of the facts that would make them unequal with respect to their fellow deliberators. In this way, once again, they are placed in circumstances structured so that the outcomes of their choices are fair.

Motivational Constraints

In addition to the constraints on knowledge, the contractors labor under two motivational constraints. We know already that the contractors are motivated to construct principles of justice they believe will maximally advance their conception of the good (whatever it turns out to be). However, the following constraints on motivation guide this task. Both of these constraints limit the pool of candidate principles, the first by constraining a type of consideration (envy) in the original position, and the second by alerting the contractors to the limits on motivation that can be expected from citizens in civil society.

Mutual Disinterest

Mutual disinterest signifies that the contractors are unconcerned with how well or badly *others* will do under candidate principles of justice. In one sense we already know this because we know that the contractors are rationally pursuing *their own* idea of the good. They are not interested in the extent to which others succeed in realizing their alternative conceptions. Thus, when considering candidate principles Rawls requires that contractors concern themselves *only* with how well they themselves would do and not consider how well they do *in comparison with* others. As a contractor I seek to do the best for myself even if that means that others do better than I do. For example, let us suppose that I want more rather than fewer apples but the only way I can maximize my share of apples (say, getting two rather than one) is to allow that everyone else around me gets more (say, four). I could opt for another scheme where I get only one apple and everyone else gets only one as well, but this would be to judge my share in comparison with others and to take less just so others get less as well.

The idea of mutual disinterest is to prevent the contractors from thinking in this way. In short, the contractors are not *envious* of others.

Rawls's reasoning here relies on the technical claim that it would be irrational for the contractors to minimize their own well-being for no advantage to themselves. Rational agents are agents who maximize their well-being and sacrificing well-being to satisfy a psychological impulse is irrational on this standard. Much rests on this seemingly minor constraint. At this stage it is not necessary to explore the technical details of Rawls's argument. We can just be satisfied with noting that Rawls understands rationality in a standard economic sense where envy is regarded as an irrational impulse. Allowing envy a place in the contractors' reasoning would permit principles that would result in *everyone* being worse off than they need to be (our simple apple example shows how this might happen). One possible difficulty for Rawls is that even if we agree that the contractors are not envious, citizens often are. We are sometimes deeply concerned with how we compare with our neighbors. This problem touches on the issue of inequalities in welfare, which is a main theme of Rawls's work, a theme that we will return to again and again.

Strains of Commitment

This next constraint on motivation is easier to explain and defend. The contractors are agreeing on principles to govern the basic institutions of society and they are relying on rationality as their guide in their deliberations. One consideration is that whatever principles they agree to must be ones that it is possible for ordinary citizens to abide by. It would be irrational to enter into an agreement that you believed citizens had a great incentive to break. In other words, an agreement must be one to which citizens can commit themselves. If the strain of committing oneself is too great, if the sacrifice required to keep to the agreement is too heavy, then citizens will defect from the agreement. An absence of agreement is the worst of all outcomes. The contractors know this and so in choosing between candidate principles they take into account the strains of commitment. For example, suppose the contractors agreed to allow limited forms of slavery. Suppose an annual lottery drafted five percent of the adult population into sweatshops (to make it "fair"). Now, if, as we are supposing, the principles that allow this situation define justice for this society, all citizens, including the draftees, should commit to these principles. However, the unlucky draftees will have a great incentive to defect from the agreement and cease to abide by the principles of "justice" because obviously the strain of slavery is very great and is more of a strain than we could expect ordinary citizens to bear. As Rawls says, "They cannot enter into agreements that may have consequences they cannot accept" (TJ: 153). The strains of commitment will be too great for these citizens. An agreement that cannot be kept is no agreement at all and it would be irrational to enter into such an agreement.

Not only should the contractors be concerned about how others might have incentives to break contracts, they should also be concerned about whether they themselves (and their descendants) would be able to keep to agreements made in the original position. Rawls makes it clear that the contractors do not gamble with their freedoms and welfare even if the winning roll of the dice is very advantageous. For instance, in the sweatshop example above, the ninety-five percent of citizens who benefit from the slave labor of the few might enjoy a considerable enhancement of their welfare. However, Rawls says that "compacts of this sort exceed the capacity of human nature" (TJ: 154), and the contractors will not risk agreeing to an arrangement that exceeds their own capacities for fidelity. Moreover, Rawls requires that the contractors choose principles that will govern not only themselves but their descendants as well. In other words, they are choosing for future generations of their direct descendants. Rawls supposes that while it might be tempting to risk slavery for oneself in exchange for the life of the slaveholder it is a different matter entirely if one is risking slavery for all one's children and grandchildren.

Overall, the principles of justice selected among the candidates should "generate their own support" among citizens. They should arrange the basic institutions of society so that everyone benefits. Thus, everyone has an incentive to abide by them and internalize their imperatives. The strains of commitment are thus a significant constraint on the deliberations of the contractors. While it is uncontroversial to think that it is a matter of reason to enter into contracts that the parties have sufficient incentives to keep, it is much more controversial to require that the contractors eschew risk-taking. Indeed, it might be argued that it is rational, in some circumstances, to take significant risks if the possible benefits are large enough. We will return to this question when we examine Rawls's arguments against utilitarianism.

These then, are the epistemic and motivational constraints on the deliberations of the contractors. These constraints structure the circumstances of the contractors so that the range of their choices between possible principles falls within the set of possible fair principles. That is, they cannot choose to advantage just themselves (since they do not know where they will fall in society) and they cannot choose to risk massively disadvantaging others (because these others will defect) or risk massively disadvantaging themselves (because they must consider their descendants and their own capacity to stay true to the principles they choose). Thus, although the contractors do not seek fairness, their circumstances demand that what they choose will be fair.

METHOD OF REASONING

Now that we have looked at the epistemic and motivational constraints on the contractors' reasoning we turn to their method of reasoning. We want to know how they work with the considerations and candidate principles they are presented with. Their method of reasoning is also a constraint insofar as they are not permitted to exceed the bounds of rationality. This is not to say that what rationality demands is always obvious and clear. Indeed, there is often controversy on this very question. However, rationality does have its borders and we do need to know where Rawls draws them. The first requirement of rationality is that the principles the contractors impose meet a set of formal constraints. These are requirements of form and not of content. They tell us what the logical form or character of the principles must have to be rational. The second requirement of rationality specifies the method of reasoning the contractors use to choose between candidate principles of justice (assuming the candidate principles have met the formal requirements).

Formal Constraints of Reason

We have said all along that the contractors are to deliberate about which principles of justice should determine the division of advantages in a democratic society. We have not said anything about what is to count as a principle of justice. Here are some examples of "principles" that will *not* fall under Rawls's definition of a suitable principle.

1. Everyone is to serve Paul Voice's interests.
2. To each according to his threat advantage.

Rawls's definition will also eliminate principles that are known or understood only by a few people. It will also require that the principles chosen be supreme in the sense that they are the final court of appeal. In one way Rawls is appealing to what we ordinarily mean when we talk of principles of justice. He is just spelling out our intuitive grasp of how we understand and use certain concepts. After all, the outcomes likely to result from the application of the second "principle" above are precisely what we want to avoid when we undertake a search for principles of justice. But Rawls's constraints are more than plain old conceptual analysis. They have normative consequences insofar as they eliminate certain forms of egoism. They are an appeal to what we the readers and democratic citizens would find reasonable to impose as a guide to the logical grammar of principles of justice. Rawls thinks of these guidelines as following from the "constraints of the concept of right." We next examine four basic formal constraints of reason that Rawls identifies. They are generality, universality, publicity, and finality.

Generality. The principles to which the contractors agree should not contain proper names or "rigged definite descriptions." This would eliminate from consideration the first "principle" above because it contains a proper name. It picks out for special consideration and advantage a particular individual just in virtue of his being that person (it would be a mistake to pick him out for special disadvantages, too). The thought behind this requirement is that we enjoy our moral standing in virtue of properties and actions (properties that others may have as well and actions others may also perform) and not because we are a *particular* individual. It is not because I am Paul Voice that I deserve your moral consideration, but rather because I have certain rights or because my well-being counts.

In addition to proper names Rawls rules out definite descriptions that are obviously designed to pick out particular individuals. For example, someone might say that special advantages are due to anyone who is the author of a book on Rawls, lives in

Massachusetts, drives a Subaru, and was born in a hospital in Surrey, England. This description does not name me, but it picks me out *and* is designed to pick me out and so is rigged. Now this is not to say that a legitimate principle would not in fact pick out only me. Suppose my luck changed and a principle that accorded special advantages to the least well-off person in Massachusetts picked me out. This definite description (the least well-off person in Massachusetts) is not designed to grab a particular person known in advance and so it is admissible.

Universality. The principles should apply to all **people** "in virtue of there being moral persons." "All people" means all citizens of a particular democratic nation state. The requirement of universality means that no one is exempt from the principles and that everyone, in principle, must be capable of both understanding and acting on them. Another important consequence is that the principles must be consistent. Their requirements cannot therefore conflict without some way of resolving the conflict. If they do conflict then there will be requirements that cannot be acted on. In short, the principles should tell us how to act (or not act) and if there is a conflict between principles it should tell us how to resolve it (by giving us a priority rule for example). Thus, the universality requirement has two aspects. It tells us the scope of the principles (they apply to everyone) and it demands, as a consequence, consistency.

Publicity. The principles should be known and "explicitly recognized" by citizens. Let us assume we know that a certain religious belief is false (it was made up in someone's kitchen and we have proof of this) but we also know that people who follow this religion happen to comply with the "true" precepts of morality (precepts they would likely not accept without their false beliefs). We might argue we should encourage them in their (false) religious beliefs. However this would not meet the publicity criterion. Rawls says that the "point of the publicity condition is to have the parties evaluate conceptions of justice as publicly acknowledged and fully effective moral constitutions of social life" (TJ: 115). What is required is that citizens act justly for the right reasons; reasons they themselves recognize and acknowledge.

Ordering. The purpose of the principles of justice is to adjudicate between competing claims to the benefits and burdens of social cooperation. For the principles to effectively adjudicate requires that the principles order conflicting claims and so allow citizens to determine what justice requires.

Finality. The last formal constraint on the principles is the requirement that they be the final court of appeal: "There are no higher standards to which arguments in support of claims can be addressed" (TJ: 116). Rawls goes on to argue that these principles "override the demands of law and custom, and of social rules generally" (TJ: 116). This means that democratic citizens are first concerned with what justice demands of them and only then concerned with what their particular and local customs require. The requirement of finality is another point of philosophical contention. As we will see later when we examine criticisms of Rawls, some communitarians will object to the idea that justice is independent of, and stands above, the particular and the local.

Maximin Principle

In addition to the formal constraints on the principles, we need to know what substantively guides the reasoning of the contractors. Supposing there is a set of candidate principles that meet the requirements of the formal constraints on reason, how do the contractors make choices between principles? Further, what makes these choices *rational*? The answer to this question is embedded in the various considerations we have advanced so far. What we need to do is make explicit the rationality of how the contractors make choices. The maximin principle guides the selections of the parties in the original position by directing them to protect themselves against the worst possible outcomes; it requires the contractors to *maximize the minimum* outcome for themselves. We might think of this as the contractors choosing a basic structure for society in which their enemy will assign them a place. If they maximize the worst possible outcome then they avoid tragedy, although they surrender the possibility of glory as well. To understand this consider the matrix below that Rawls (TJ: 133) uses to illustrate the workings of the maximin principle (where the numbers represent money in hundred dollar amounts).

	Circumstances		
Decisions	C1	C2	C3
D1	–7	8	12
D2	–8	7	14
D3	5	6	8

It is obvious that securing the best worst outcome results from making the third decision. This is not to say that the worst outcome will eventuate of course; it is rather to say that whatever happens the contractor protects herself from the grim possibilities that the other decisions risk. Rawls offers three reasons why the maximin rule is preferred in the original position. First, the parties, as we have already specified, do not take risks. This is an especially acute consideration since the veil of ignorance makes the calculation of probabilities very difficult and exaggerates the uncertainties the contractors face. The maximin principle reflects the conservative attitude of the contractors. Second, the contractors care most deeply about their conception of the good. This means that they are concerned, in the first instance, to secure circumstances that will allow them to advance their conception. Any advantages they might gain above this minimum are discounted if they risk their freedom to live their lives according to their own fundamental values. Lastly, the maximin rule defends against seriously bad outcomes that will diminish the life prospects of citizens to a considerable degree. We should remember that the contractors are choosing not only for themselves but also for their direct descendants. They will not choose principles that may subject them to an intolerable existence.

Overall, these three reasons combine to make the maximin principle the guide for the contractors' choices. So Rawls's claim here is that free, equal, and rational persons under a veil of ignorance and motivationally constrained in the ways described above use the maximin principle as their method of reasoning in the original position.

THE OBJECTS OF DELIBERATION

Now that we have set out the methods of reasoning the contractors employ in the original position, we can turn our attention to the objects of their deliberation and raise the question: What are they deliberating *about*?

Basic Structure

The contractors, the abstract inhabitants of the original position, seek principles of justice, as we have said. What are these principles supposed to govern? This question of application is important because different theories of justice apply their principles more or less broadly. This raises the question of the *scope* of Rawls's theory. For example, the utilitarian theory of justice has a very wide scope insofar as its principles apply to and regulate all aspects of life, from relations between citizens and the state, to relations between friends, and, even, arguably, between one's present self and one's future self. Rawls's theory of justice has a much narrower scope. The principles of justice that will emerge from the contractors' deliberations will apply to and regulate what he calls the "basic structure" of society. Of course, this is not to say that Rawls thinks this is the only question of justice that can or should be asked. However, his account of justice as fairness is restricted in scope; it is thus focused on a particular problem of justice. What is the basic structure and why is it so important?

The basic structure governs "the way in which the major social institutions distribute fundamental rights and duties and determine the division of advantages from social cooperation" (TJ: 6). Let us begin by assuming that citizens cooperate in society for a shared advantage. Then the question naturally arises about how that advantage is distributed. However, knowing how the advantages are distributed does not tell us a great deal unless we know the mechanisms by which they are distributed. These mechanisms are the "major social institutions," in particular, the political, social, and economic institutions of society. These institutions are major for two connected reasons. First, they have a normative function by assigning rights and duties, that is, they set up a framework of "oughts" that (ideally) govern the interactions between citizens. Take, for example, the institution of private property in the means of production (like factories for example). This institution assigns rights of ownership to citizens in the property itself and in the profit that is derived from its use (although both these rights are limited in many ways in actual liberal democratic states). Citizens thus ought to be allowed ownership in the means of production, and other citizens ought to respect that right where appropriate providing ownership of the means of production is compatible with the principles of justice. Second, this institution is maintained by the threat of coercion. The state uses its monopoly on coercive power to enforce the normative requirements of the institution. Now clearly, an institution like private property in the means of production is very important when considering how the benefits and burdens of social cooperation are distributed. The legal system is another institution that Rawls mentions, as an example, when describing the basic structure. For instance, it is obvious that how a legal system defines a person with legal standing is crucial to how citizens make claims on each other. What makes these political, economic, and social institutions basic is their profound effect on the lives of citizens. These institutions fit together into a system that governs the day-to-day interactions between citizens in the most fundamental way. This is why Rawls calls it a structure; it provides the framework within which citizens interact with the state and each other.

Another sense in which these institutions are basic is that they are public institutions regulated by the state. An economic system of competitive markets is public in the sense that citizens (ought to) have free access to the market and its benefits, and the conditions that permit the free market are maintained by state agencies. Likewise, marriage is a public institution and, for Rawls, part of the basic structure. Marriage is regulated by the state (it determines who can and cannot marry, for example) and it is public in the sense that all citizens are governed by the laws of marriage. Marriage is also basic because it reaches into citizens' lives and is important in determining how a person fares in her life. Now, it is important to emphasize the public character of the basic structure because the principles of justice that the contractors will agree to do not apply to private institutions like churches and clubs. One crucial way private institutions differ from public ones is that membership in private institutions is voluntary whereas, for Rawls, citizens are born into a particular set of basic institutions and do not choose to be members of their societies. Now as citizens we can, in principle at least, emigrate, of course. However, the contractors, when deliberating about the principles of justice, view their society as a closed system in which citizens enter at birth and exit only with death. This abstraction simplifies their deliberations and forces them to reach agreement on principles they will *have to* abide by. So, although churches, for example, can have profound effects on people's lives, they do not count as basic for Rawls because they are voluntary associations and so citizens can choose whether to be governed by their rules and choose whether or not to bear the burdens of, or take advantage of, their activities.

This distinction between the public and the private is notoriously problematic. For one current example of a dispute about the boundaries between the public and the private one only has to look to the issue of marriage in the United States. On one side of the argument stand those who, recognizing the profound affects of the institution of marriage (its "basicness"), argue that the state should allow same-sex couples to marry. They argue that the state should change the rules that are used to govern this basic institution. Others have argued that the state should "disestablish" marriage, in other words, that marriage should become a private matter between citizens and not be regulated by the state. More commonly, philosophers argue about the extent to which the state should interfere in the life of the family—they raise questions concerning what is private and what is public about the family. For example, in Britain beating one's children is now illegal. Is the way parents punish their children a private or public matter? These and many arguments about the divide between public and private need not detain us for very long. Rawls relies on a distinction between the public and private without specifying where, precisely, to draw the line. In fact he does not need to draw this line precisely. His point is that the principles of justice apply to the basic structure and not to private associations, wherever the line between the private and the public is finally drawn.

The basic structure has the following three features: First, it is a set of institutions (political, economic, and social) that fit together to form a system. Second, these institutions regulate interactions between citizens in matters that have a profound affect on their life prospects (how well they fare in life) and lastly, the basic structure refers to public and not private institutions. We need to add another important point before moving on. Rawls refers to the basic structure as the background against which citizens conduct their lives. This means that the basic structure forms the framework within which citizens make choices. In many ways this framework or background is invisible to citizens; it is only when we are stopped from doing what we want that the constraints that the basic structure imposes become evident to us. For as long as we move along unimpeded, the basic structure recedes from view. However, there is a more important point lurking in Rawls's choice of the word "background" when talking about the basic structure. Not only do the major institutions constrain our choices, they also *shape* our "wants and aspirations." What we come to want is, in part, a function of how the basic structure steers and guides us towards certain values. We are born into a particular society (not one we have chosen) that already has a basic structure with all the attendant values that such a structure rests on. These values become embedded in our view of the world. This is not to say that we are hostage to them—we are not. However, Rawls is keen to point out the importance of the basic structure in shaping our outlook on the world. The basic structure is not just a set of rules; it is also a window on the world that offers a particular perspective. This final, fourth point emphasizes the centrality of the basic structure for the question of justice. A just society will be one that has a just basic structure. Therefore, it is clear why Rawls says that the principles of justice apply, in the first instance, to the basic structure. It is this structure, this set of institutions, that is to be governed and regulated by the principles that the contractors agree to.

Primary Goods

The basic structure is the object of deliberation in the sense that it is the structure to which the principles of justice are applied. Thus the principles of justice distribute the benefits and burdens that the basic structure (the major social institutions) generates. This raises the question of how we are going to measure and calculate these benefits and burdens. It is clearly important that we have some instrument of measurement in order to be able to tell how candidate principles of justice differ in their distributions when applied to the basic structure. We also need to be able to tell how individual citizens fare and, more importantly, how citizens fare when compared to one another. Rawls's answer to this question is what he calls the "social primary goods." The way the basic structure of society is arranged determines the extent of the social primary goods and how they are distributed between citizens.

Let us begin by adopting the point of view of the contractors in the original position. They stand behind the veil of ignorance and so have to make choices about principles of justice without knowing their particular conception of the good. As they review possible principles of justice, they are trying to determine how well they (and their descendants) are going to do living in a society effectively governed by those principles. They are ignorant of what they take the good to be, and therefore they cannot tell to what extent they will be able to realize their particular conception of the good. Thus they need another measure to adjudicate between principles. Citizens in a democratic society also need to make assessments concerning their own well-being. They also need to have a basis on which to make claims against the state and its institutions. As we will discuss later, such claims will concern needs that they have *as citizens* and not claims concerning needs they have only from within the private perspective of their particular "comprehensive doctrines." This entails that the social primary goods are going to have to be the sorts of goods that address the needs of citizens independently of any particular conception of the good. In other words, the social primary goods must be *political* in character. Finally, from our point of view in assessing Rawls's theory of justice we need to be able to make interpersonal comparisons between citizens so as to make judgments about how a Rawlsian theory of justice stands up against alternative theories of justice.

Rawls identifies the following goods as the social and material primary goods: rights, liberties, opportunities, income and wealth, and the bases of self-respect. These goods are distinct from the "natural" primary goods such as "health and vigor, intelligence and imagination" (TJ: 54). Although these latter goods are very important, of course, they are not goods that can be directly distributed by the basic structure: they are "not under control" of society (TJ: 54).

We can divide the list of primary goods into three parts: (a) rights, liberties, and opportunities, (b) income and wealth, and (c) the bases of self-respect. Rights, liberties, and opportunities are regulated by the rules that institutions set down. For example, a right to private ownership in the means of production permits such ownership (and the benefits arising from it). It forbids nonowners from alienating such property without the uncoerced agreement of the owner. This right also specifies a freedom to own property and a freedom from interference from the state and other citizens. Opportunities are occasions when rights and liberties can be exercised. Rawls has in mind opportunities to choose an occupation, to move about freely, and the opportunity to hold political office. These primary goods are available to citizens in virtue of the system of rules that institutions of the basic structure impose and enforce. Income and wealth are material resources that the basic structure distributes through mechanisms such as the competitive market, benefits paid directly to citizens by the state, and exchanges of income and wealth between citizens, for example, inheritances. The final kind of primary good is the "bases of self-respect." In the *Theory of Justice* Rawls describes this good as "perhaps the most important" (TJ: 348). Rawls is not saying that the basic structure distributes the psychological state of feelings of self-worth, because clearly this is not something that can be given out like rights and income. However, he does assert that the basic structure provides the foundation on which citizens can come to have self-respect (and respect for their fellow citizens). He argues that when the basic structure is just, or at least nearly just, then citizens will have reason to respect themselves and others. Thus he takes respect to be a foundational value both morally and politically and he therefore includes it in his list of primary goods. One final point is in order here. Rawls does not claim that his list of primary goods is closed and thus final. Again, we should distinguish between the analytical tool that Rawls offers and the specific content he gives when using the tool. For example, we can disagree about what should be put behind the veil of ignorance while still agreeing that the veil is a useful analytical tool for ensuring fair outcomes. Likewise, we can disagree about the list of primary goods while still agreeing on the need for such a list.

What makes these goods *primary*? They are primary because they are goods that democratic citizens need and require in order to follow a rational plan of life, that is, successfully pursue their conception of the good. They are the kinds of goods needed by citizens in a democratic state *whatever* their conception of the good happens to be. Thus whether one is an observant Jew or a secular liberal, one needs some basic rights and liberties and some income and wealth to fully live out the life that one desires. They are *practical* means towards the reasonable ends of citizens in a democratic state.

I have emphasized the connection between the primary goods and the needs of democratic citizens because Rawls does not mean his list of primary goods to be taken as a list of goods satisfying universal human needs. This list of primary goods is drawn up subsequent to setting out his normative account of the democratic citizen, which we examined earlier. Citizens conceived of as free, equal, and rational have needs that can be satisfied, in an initial and minimal way, by some measure of the primary goods. In this way the primary goods are political. They underpin the various private conceptions of the good citizens in a democratic state hold, but they are not themselves private goods. The primary goods, therefore, are part of what Rawls calls a "thin" rather than a "thick" theory of the good—a distinction that will be important in his later work.

The primary goods are a measure of citizens' expectations over the course of their lives. The greater their share of primary goods, then the better they fare since it is with these goods that they can realize their hopes and satisfy their wants. Of course, there is no guarantee that citizens will use their share of the primary goods wisely or that they will not suffer some deficiency of intelligence or motivation that will frustrate their wants. However, for Rawls and his understanding of justice what matters is that citizens have some share of primary goods that is fair and meets their needs as citizens.

Let us now return to the contractors in the original position. From their perspective the list of primary goods gives them the measure they need to adjudicate between competing sets of principles of justice. Recall that they labor under the veil of ignorance. Consequently they can only choose principles based on their assessment of how they will fare in society and so they will judge principles of justice by weighing their share of the primary goods: the greater the better, the less the worse.

These, then, are the objects of deliberation for the contractors in the original position—the basic structure and the primary goods that the basic structure distributes. The principles of justice will govern the basic structure and thereby determine how the primary goods are distributed.

The Principles

THE THREE MAIN GROUNDS FOR THE PRINCIPLES

Everything is now in place for the contractors, our representatives in the original position, to reason and deliberate towards principles of justice. In this section we will briefly examine the grounds that underpin their deliberations. The contractors are conceived of as rational, mutually disinterested with a sense of justice. They understand themselves as in the circumstances of justice (objective and subjective) and understand the formal constraints that apply to the candidate principles (the constraints of universality, generality, publicity, ordering, and finality). Lastly, they find themselves behind a veil of ignorance, subject to the strains of commitment, and operating with the maximin principle as their guide in their deliberations.

The three main grounds for the principles the contractors agree to emerge from the conditions and constraints set out in the previous paragraph. To further appreciate these grounds, we should put ourselves in the shoes of the contractors. First, we understand this much about ourselves: we have wants and interests (we have a conception of the good) and we seek the means to satisfy these wants and pursue these interests (we are rational). However, we do not know what our interests are due to the veil of ignorance. Thus, we reason that we need a basic structure governed by a rule that provides for the greatest amount of freedom so that whatever our conception of the good we are free to pursue it. For example, choosing a theocracy would be foolish since we do not know whether we share the beliefs a theocracy would impose on citizens. The wider the scope of liberty in society the greater the chance will be that our conception of the good, our interests and wants, will be satisfied. So the first ground for our deliberations as contractors will be to secure as much freedom as possible for ourselves. The contractors treasure liberty not because liberty has intrinsic value to them, but for instrumental, rational reasons.

Second, as contractors we know that liberty is not enough to give us a chance of pursuing and satisfying our idea of the good. We need not only to be free but also to have the *means* to achieve our ends. Although some conceptions of the good can be realized with minimal resources many, probably most, require some measure of resources to be successfully pursued. We also know that we will have a particular conception of the good requiring a determinate minimum of resources. Therefore, it will be essential to secure the most favorable material circumstances for ourselves so that we can advance our idea of the good whatever it turns out to be.

Third, our choice of principles will be guided by the maximin principle. This principle guides us in circumstances where we have very little information. The veil of ignorance ensures that we know nothing about our particular place in society. It follows that we have no objective grounds to calculate probabilities. If we did, then it might be rational to gamble that we would be beneficiaries of a society that rewarded some citizens with extensive liberties and great resources but denied them to others. As contractors we want to do the best we can for ourselves and our descendants. A gamble might be a rational course of action, depending on the probabilities of success and the rewards of success. However, once again, since the contractors are entirely ignorant of their place in society, they know only the possible rewards but nothing of the probability that they would be the beneficiary of these rewards.

In summary, the bases for deliberations between the contractors in the original position are as follows: They seek to maximize their share of liberty as well as to maximize their share of the society's material resources, and they are highly conservative in assessing probabilities.

A STATEMENT OF THE TWO PRINCIPLES

We can start with a statement of the two principles agreed to by the contractors. Rawls sets them out as follow (TJ: 266):

> First Principle: Each person is to have an equal right to the most extensive total system of basic equal liberties compatible with a similar system of liberty for all.
>
> Second Principle: Social and economic inequalities are to be arranged so that they are both: (a) to the greatest benefit of the least advantaged, consistent with the just savings principle, and (b) attached to offices and positions open to all under conditions of fair equality of opportunity.

The first principle is the greatest equal liberty principle and the second is the difference principle plus the equal opportunity principle. These principles distribute the primary goods; rights and liberties in the first principle and opportunities, income, and wealth in the second principle. The primary good of self-respect can be thought to supervene on the successful application of these two principles to the basic structure. We need to explain four aspects of the two principles. Explain (a) the meaning of each of the principles, (b) explain why the contractors agree to them, (c) explain the ordering of the principles, and (d) view the principles from the perspective of citizens in a democratic society.

The Greatest Equal Liberty Principle

The greatest equal liberty principle largely explains itself. The basic structure of society is to be organized so that every citizen enjoys, and is assured of, the widest possible extent of freedom. This freedom is to be defined by and protected by a right to liberty. The second part of the first principle is necessary because the extent of citizens' freedoms is bounded by the freedoms of other citizens. For example, my right to privacy can only be realized if your freedom is, to some degree, limited. Rawls offers a list of the types of liberties he has in mind in the first principle (TJ: 53):

> political liberty (the right to vote and hold public office) and freedom of speech and assembly; liberty of conscience and freedom of thought; freedom of the person, which includes freedom from psychological oppression and physical assault and dismemberment (integrity of the person); the right to hold personal property and freedom from arbitrary arrest and seizure as defined by the concept of the rule of law.

This principle should be attractive to the contractors. We know they treasure freedom (albeit on purely instrumental grounds) and that they seek to maximize their share of it so as to efficiently pursue their conception of the good. However, they also know that their fellow contractors are seeking to maximize their share too. In a strategic situation such as this, and given the constraints of the veil of ignorance, it is rational to opt for the first principle since it offers the greatest freedom no matter what one's eventual position in society turns out to be. The first principle results in a basic structure that distributes liberty equally between citizens. This principle captures both the values of freedom as well as equality, values central to a democratic society. However, the contractors do not aim to promote these values. They are not concerned to promote any particular values because they are prevented from knowing what values they subscribe to. Nevertheless, the situation constructed in the original position forces them to choose the values of political equality and freedom. In other words, Rawls constructs a *fair* initial situation where the contingencies of history, society, and the happenstances of individuals have been removed from view. In this situation of fairness, freedom and political equality emerge as the values that rational agents seeking to advance their own interests would choose. Insofar as we, the readers, imaginatively identify with the contractors (accept the constraints of the situation and agree with its fairness) then we, too. will embrace liberty and political equality as the foundational values of a democratic society. Finally, from the point of view of citizens in a democratic state, the first principle recognizes and protects their self-conception as free and equal agents. The first principle thus resonates with the self-understanding that citizens have in a democratic state and achieves reflective equilibrium; it is a principle that coheres with their values and the facts as they understand them; most importantly though, the reasoning of the contractors stands as a *justification* of the first principle for democratic citizens. We can now turn to the second principle.

The Equal Opportunity Principle and the Difference Principle

The values contained in the equal opportunity principle are familiar democratic and liberal values and echo the normative commitments of Rawls's liberal predecessors. The difference principle is more innovative, controversial, and challenging. The first principle concerns the distribution of rights and liberties and achieving political equality, whereas the second principle is concerned instead with the distribution of the material primary goods, such as income, wealth, and opportunities.

In the first part of the difference principle, Rawls speaks of the distribution of *inequalities*. Egalitarians will balk at this assumption. Why should citizens not enjoy material equality (welfare equality or resource equality) as well as political equality? Moreover, would not the contractors opt for material equality since they reason behind the veil of ignorance? These are reasonable inquiries but they neglect the reasoning of the contractors when they consider the distribution of the material primary goods.

In answer to the egalitarian we note that the contractors are concerned only to advance their own interests and are not concerned with how they well they do when compared to others. They are strictly rational in the sense that they seek their own advantage. We also know that the contractors have sociological and economic knowledge so they understand the basics of how economies are likely to work. With this is mind we can understand their reasoning. To start with, they will not settle for a principle that favors some but not others, since they could be among the disadvantaged rather than the advantaged. This will lead them towards a principle of equal distribution in which everyone is to have an equal share of the material primary goods. However, this will not be the end of their deliberations. They will know that the quantity of material goods in an economy is dynamic and that some economic arrangements provide incentives that increase the overall level of material goods (income, wealth, and opportunities). This consideration is then tied to the further thought that as long as the contractors' gain from an unequal distribution of material primary goods, then it is rational for them to agree to such an unequal distribution. However, if there is no gain, then there should be an equal distribution. Thus, Rawls argues there should be an equal distribution of material primary goods *unless* an unequal distribution benefits the least advantaged.

This raises the question of why Rawls picks out the least advantaged as his measure of who benefits. The answer is to be found in the reasoning of the contractors. As they make choices between candidate principles, they apply the maximin rule which, as we have already discussed, directs the contractors to opt for the *best-worst* outcome. If there are inequalities between citizens, there is always someone or some group who is the worst off. The outcome contractors will want to avoid is one where *they* are the worst off. One way they can achieve this is by choosing an egalitarian principle of equal distribution. However, if the worst off in an unequal distribution of material primary goods is better off than she would be on an equal distribution, then it would be rational for her to choose to be the worst off in such a distribution. The matrix below explains this complex piece of reasoning more clearly. The numbers refer to bundles of material primary goods.

	Society		
	One	Two	Three
Person			
John	5	3	7
Jane	5	8	8

John, who is the worst off in Society Three, is better off than he is in Society One where everyone receives an equal share of the primary goods. From the point of view of the contractors this is all that matters: being better off is what instrumentally rational agents seek to be. Thus, John avoids the worst outcome for himself in Society Two and avoids the better but not the best outcome in Society One, and achieves the best outcome for himself in Society Three. We should remember that the contractors do not know their place in society and so they are not choosing in the way John does. They understand they have a chance of being anyone in society. However, the maximin principle demands that they focus on the worst possible outcome and so they choose principles *as if* they were John, that is, as if they were the least-advantaged member of society. This explains how a principle of justice that results in social and economic inequalities can be the outcome of a rational choice in the original position; *the inequalities are to everyone's advantage.*

Therefore, inequalities are justified as long as the least-advantaged are better off than they would be under an equal distribution of primary goods. In general, economic arrangements must be viewed through the eyes of the worst off in society, taking their perspective as primary. The only proviso Rawls allows to this rule is the consideration of the claims of future generations. He introduces the notion of a "just savings principle" that captures the idea that the "present generation is bound to respect the claims of its successors" (TJ: 251). Rawls does not specify exactly what should be set aside for the benefit of future generations but argues that the contractors would include such a principle, partly on the grounds that they are choosing for their descendants and not only for themselves.

The second part of the second principle concerns the distribution of opportunities to occupy the offices and positions of political, economic, and social power and influence in society. This part of the second principle states that if there are inequalities in income and wealth attached to positions of power and influence, then these positions must be open to all citizens under conditions of equal opportunity. In other words, the advantages associated with an unequal share of primary goods should not result in unequal access to "offices and positions"; all citizens should have a fair shot at occupying these positions. This is the familiar equal opportunity principle that democrats and liberals subscribe to. At this juncture Rawls is concerned that differences in material resources will result in some citizens being unable to fairly compete for positions of authority, prestige, and wealth. Thus, inequalities are allowed only to the extent that equal opportunity is maintained. It is simple enough to see why the contractors place this proviso on the difference principle. They have reason to want the chance to occupy positions of power and so they have reason to equalize the opportunities to do so. They also have reason to want to be the best off in society (and not just the least well off) and therefore they want these, and all other positions, to be open to fair competition.

From the point of view of citizens the second principle recognizes that they have "rational plans of life" and thus have need of the material resources that would enable them to realize such plans. It is not enough that they have freedoms and political equality. They also require a share of a society's resources to make use of their freedom to pursue their conceptions of the good and to make use of their political equality as citizens. These resources are thus essential for their private lives as subjects and their public lives as citizens. The second principle is also a justification of material inequalities between citizens. In essence, citizens are asked to accept these inequalities on the grounds that they are better off than they would be under an equal distribution and that they are not disadvantaged in their opportunities. If these provisos are not met then citizens are justified in arguing for an egalitarian distribution of income and wealth.

THE ORDERING OF THE PRINCIPLES

Rawls sets out two principles that cover rights and liberties, and opportunities, income, and wealth. Now, obviously these principles can come into conflict with one another. For example, we can imagine a situation where political *inequality* results in greater overall material welfare. Perhaps some members of society are denied their rights of association and are thereby denied the opportunity to form labor unions and consequently are unable to challenge their working conditions. It is possible as a consequence that, *overall*, society does better, which would mean that there is a collective benefit to withholding some persons' rights (although this benefit is unevenly distributed so that those whose rights have been abridged are worse off). Another possible outcome could be that even those who are denied their rights do better than before, that is, from the point of view of their material welfare. In this instance the collective benefit is distributed so that even the least-advantaged improve their share of the material primary goods.

Which of the principles should prevail when they conflict? This is the priority problem and Rawls solves it by arguing that the first principle should be satisfied before the second principle. The technical term he uses to describe this ordering of the principles is "lexical." The principles are lexically ordered so that the greatest equal liberty principle has priority. It should be met and satisfied before the difference principle and before the principle of equal opportunity, which are also lexically ordered, the former taking precedence over the latter. In the two cases outlined in the previous paragraph the first one is easily dealt with. The contractors will not choose an ordering of principles that make some citizens worse off just so that the rest of society is better off. This conclusion rests on two considerations. First, the contractors understand they may be the victims of such a distribution rather than the beneficiaries. Second, they consider the strains of commitment and understand that those whose rights have been abridged have incentives not to abide by the principles of justice. The contractors do not select principles citizens have a strong incentive to disobey, as we have seen. This case makes clear why the contractors would not sacrifice rights for gains in material welfare.

The second case is more challenging because its assumption is that everyone benefits, in terms of material welfare, from the abridgment of rights and liberties, even the worst off would gain. Why should rights and liberties have priority in this instance? Why would the contractors choose to be worse off than they need to be? What is so essential about rights and liberties that they always trump material welfare? (Rawls allows that if the material circumstances of society were to drastically change and dip below a certain level then rights could be abridged, but only with the aim of eventually restoring rights and liberties. Anyhow, for the modern democratic societies he has in mind, this allowance does not apply). To understand why the contractors give priority to the first principle we need to reflect on their self-conception as free and equal agents. In addition to conceiving of themselves as free and equal, they also have a higher-order interest in realizing this self-conception. This means they have a higher-order interest in exercising their liberty in pursuit of their conception of the good, and being equal members of a political community. Furthermore, it is in exercising their liberties and in their political equality that they gain respect for themselves, earn the respect of others, and come to respect their fellow citizens. In other words, the primary good of self-respect emerges from the application of the first principle. Thus, the contractors discount increases in material welfare when these are purchased at the expense of rights and liberties. The contractors subordinate material welfare (providing it is available at some minimal level required for a democratic society) to the realization of themselves as democratic citizens. In the next section we will discuss further the lexical ordering of the principles and the priority Rawls gives to liberties and rights. For now, it is sufficient to note that the two principles are strictly ordered according to a rule that demands the satisfaction of the first before the satisfaction of the second.

THE UTILITARIAN ALTERNATIVE

We have examined how the contractors in the original position reason towards the two principles of justice. However, even if we are in agreement with their reasoning, the argument for the two principles is not yet made. We are asked to imagine the contractors choosing between candidate principles. Even if some principles meet the prerequisites and requirements of the original position, it does not follow that these are the *best* principles to choose. In other words, we have to show not only that the contractors choose the two principles, but also that they choose them over other candidate principles. Obviously it is not possible for Rawls to canvass all possible alternatives and show these are inadequate when compared to the two principles. Instead, Rawls focuses his attention on a short list of well-known alternatives to the contractarian approach. The most significant of these alternatives is utilitarianism.

In his analysis Rawls does not offer an argument against utilitarianism *as such*, rather he asks whether the contractors would choose utilitarian principles of justice in the original position. In other words, he asks whether the *normative* principles that utilitarians advocate would be the choice of the contractors. Rawls does not directly tackle the underlying justification usually offered for utilitarianism, namely, a naturalistic understanding of the good. Instead, given the contractarian understanding of what counts as a justification of normative principles of justice which is agreement in a suitably defined initial situation, then the question posed is whether utilitarian principles would be chosen in such a situation.

A utilitarian argues that principles of justice, when applied to the basic structure of society, should maximize utility (understood by Rawls as the "satisfaction of desire"). Rawls distinguishes between two interpretations of utilitarianism, classical and average. The former interpretation argues that we should maximize the sum total of satisfaction of the society overall. The latter interpretation argues that we should apply principles that maximize the average utility or satisfaction for citizens. The following simple example will illustrate the differences between these two interpretations of utilitarianism. The classical version is indifferent to a choice between a society of five people enjoying a level of satisfaction measured at four on a five-point scale and a society of ten people enjoying a level of satisfaction of two on the same scale. This is because the total satisfaction is the same for both societies. However, the average version is sensitive to these differences because the average utility enjoyed by citizens in each of these societies is very different. The contractors would prefer the average interpretation over the classical one since they seek to maximize *their own* welfare; they do not seek to maximize the general welfare. There are technical details here that I have skipped over but need not detain us since most of Rawls's arguments against the utilitarian choice in the original position apply to both interpretations.

Four Arguments against Utilitarianism

The first argument against the utilitarian alternative is a general one. Rawls says that the mode of reasoning the utilitarian employs "does not take seriously the distinction between persons" (TJ: 24). What matters on a utilitarian view is the maximization of some good (happiness, satisfaction, and so on) across society as a whole. This way of thinking about the good is familiar to us all because we as individuals often think of our own lives in the same way. For example, we suffer through a statistics course at college because we want to meet the prerequisites for an upper-level psychology course of our choice. Our general tendency is to postpone the opportunities for present pleasures for greater future satisfactions. Indeed, it is rational to concern oneself with how satisfactions are distributed across one's life and not to privilege the present over the future (other than factoring in the certainty of a present satisfaction with the probability of a future one). Impulsive people are precisely those who do not think rationally when calculating the spread of satisfactions across their lives. Rawls claims that utilitarianism takes this model of rationality, which properly belongs to an individual's concern with her life, and applies it to society as a whole. Thus the utilitarian argues that in the same way that it is rational for an individual not to privilege the present stage of her life over her life as a whole, he argues it is rational not to privilege individuals over society as a whole. What is important for the utilitarian is the total sum of satisfactions across individuals and not what particular satisfactions individuals enjoy.

However, the contractors are concerned with what particular satisfactions they receive in society; more precisely, they are concerned to advance *their* conception of the good. Furthermore, they are "mutually disinterested" and so they are not concerned with how others do. In short, they conceive of themselves as individuals who have particular sets of interests and a higher-order interest in realizing and achieving the satisfaction of these interests. This raises two major issues we can briefly touch on here. First, the utilitarian supposes that there is a common understanding of the good, and that it is possible to make comparisons between citizens by this common measure. Thus, for a utilitarian, it does not matter who, in particular, one is in society, only that the spread of satisfaction is maximized. For the contractors, though, it does matter who, in particular, one is because they conceive of themselves as being determinate persons with particular interests, though, of course, they do not know what these are. Therefore, the contractors do take seriously the differences between themselves and their fellow citizens even though the veil of ignorance denies them knowledge of what these differences are.

Second, if we impose the constraints of the original position on a utilitarian she will have no grounds for choosing between possible basic structures. In particular, if we impose the constraint that she is mutually disinterested, and chooses from a strictly rational point of view, then she has no basis for making such a choice. In order to make such a choice she would want to work out the probability of being a particular person in a society governed by a candidate basic structure. However, the veil of ignorance prevents her from making this calculation—she could be anyone. The fact that she could be anyone is not the same thing as an equal probability of being anyone. There is simply no basis on which to make probability calculations of this kind whatsoever. Therefore, if it matters who one is and one cannot figure out the probability of being a particular person (or member of a particular representative group of persons), then the utilitarian in the original position will not know how to make choices except to choose the society with the highest average utility and gamble that she does better than she would have done in a different society. However, as we have seen, the contractors are not gamblers.

The arguments that follow this general claim against utilitarianism rely on the particulars of the set-up of the original position. The second argument rests on the requirement of finality for the principles of justice. As we have seen, the finality requirement demands that any principle of justice adopted by the contractors be one that they, as citizens, will be able to abide by. Not only does Rawls expect citizens to be able to abide by the principles of justice they adopt, he also expects that these principles will "generate their own support." This means that citizens will come to abide by the principles *because* they are just, and not merely because they serve the interests of citizens. Rawls argues that utilitarianism fails the test of finality. He claims that citizens in a society governed by utilitarian principles may be required to sacrifice their own long term interests for the common good and would therefore have strong incentives to defect from the requirements of principles. Utilitarianism exceeds the strains of commitment. Rawls states (TJ: 155):

> Even when we are less fortunate, we are to accept the greater advantages of others as a sufficient reason for lower expectations over the whole course of our life. This is surely an extreme demand. In fact, when society is conceived as a system of cooperation designed to advance the good of its members, it seems quite incredible that some citizens should be expected, on the basis of political principles, to accept still lower prospects of life for others.

In order for the strains of commitment not to weigh too heavily on citizens in a society governed by utilitarian principles the utilitarian has to rely on assumptions about people's capacity to identify with the interests of others. Rawls finds these assumptions dubious. In the quotation above, he is clear on this point. Rawls argues that the degree of identification needs to be strong enough to sustain a lifetime of lowered life prospects for those who end up worse off in a utilitarian society. No such assumptions are needed for the two principles. In fact, the principles are arrived at without any assumptions about sympathies or identifications with the interests of others (except for one's descendants). Additionally, we have already demonstrated that it is not rational to enter into agreements that one is not persuaded others will keep. Rawls's charging utilitarianism with not meeting the requirements of the strains of commitment alerts us again to this principle of rational agreement.

According to Rawls the two principles of justice fare better on this score than utilitarianism. The application of the maximin principle serves to avert the worst outcomes. The contractors ensure that they will not be called on to make significant sacrifices of the kind Rawls alleges utilitarianism might demand. Thus the two principles meet the requirement of the strains of commitment. Furthermore, the principles take seriously the idea of society as a *cooperative* enterprise. In a well-ordered society, everyone benefits from the application of the principles; no one is worse off *just so* others can be better off. Finally, since everyone benefits in this way it follows that everyone has an incentive to maintain the agreement thus assuring the rationality of entering into it in the first place. For these reasons the contractors will favor the two principles over the utilitarian alternative.

The third argument against utilitarianism is the claim that it fails to give the proper *status* to rights and liberties. Rawls privileges rights over the good. This is reflected in the contractors' choice of the first principle and the lexical priority they give it. As previously, shown this lexical priority entails that increases in welfare cannot be traded for fewer rights and liberties. Therefore, rights and liberties have a special standing in Rawls's account of justice. A utilitarian is concerned only to maximize the good—the total or average utility. As it concerns rights and liberties the utilitarian has two approaches that are consistent with maximizing the good: either to deny any special status to rights and liberties or to argue that they are important only *because* they help maximize the good. At this juncture we can proceed to construct an argument against the former approach from the standpoint of the contractors. They are concerned to advance their conceptions of the good and so they treasure the freedoms and rights that will allow them to achieve this; whatever their conception turns out to be. This concern is anchored in their self-conception as free and equal persons and their higher-order interest in realizing this self-conception. Ergo, the contractors will dismiss the utilitarian position because it gives no special standing to rights and liberties. However, the alternative utilitarian approach that privileges rights and liberties because of their utility-maximizing value is more challenging. For instance, such a utilitarian might argue that allowing people the freedom to explore alternative ways of living and protecting their rights of free expression serve the long-term interests (utility) of society as a whole (John Stuart Mill, for example, argued along these lines).

The first of Rawls's two arguments against utilitarianism turned on the finality requirement whereas the present argument and the fourth one below turn on the publicity requirement. This formal condition of publicity, as discussed earlier, demands that principles of justice should be explicitly recognized and acknowledged by citizens. On the utilitarian view we are now considering, rights and liberties have only *instrumental* value; they are useful for maximizing utility (if they indeed are—this is an empirical question, of course). However, rights that are subordinated to a principle of utility are pale versions of rights; they are not claims that trump all other claims. If the instrumental value of rights rests on citizens believing that they have a special status, then this value will evaporate as soon as it becomes public knowledge that their value is in fact instrumental rather than intrinsic. Therefore, the publicity requirement for principles of justice highlights a contradiction in the utilitarian argument. It is the contradiction between the instrumental value they assign to rights and the intrinsic value they require citizens to believe rights have. In conclusion, the utilitarian cannot offer the contractors what they demand which is rights and liberties that have a special status. The best the utilitarian can do in this regard falls foul of the publicity requirement for justice principles. Therefore, it follows that the contractors will favor the first principle and its lexical priority over the utilitarian alternative.

The fourth and final argument against utilitarianism also rests on the requirements of the publicity condition and draws on many of the issues raised in the previous three arguments. The foundation of what Rawls refers to as the "stability" of the basic structure requires principles of justice that are publicly recognized and acknowledged, that do not violate the strains of commitment, that protect and give special status to rights and liberties, and which assure that everyone benefits from their mutual cooperation. Stability is an important issue for Rawls; indeed, it is a topic that occupies much of his later work. Principles of justice that achieve the goals set out above come to "generate their own support." They thereby stabilize the basic structure and make an ongoing just society possible. In a just society, citizens act justly for the right reasons, and citizens have a commitment to preserving justice. Based on the foregoing three arguments stability cannot be achieved by the utilitarian alternative. Thus, for Rawls, utilitarianism fails the test of stability. These four arguments combine to demonstrate why the contractors would choose justice as fairness over a utilitarian alternative in the original position.

In this section we considered the principles of justice that Rawls argues should govern the distribution of primary goods by the major institutions of a democratic society. In the next section we will examine Rawls's interpretation and defense of his principles.

3. The Practicum of Justice

Realizing the Principles: The Four-Stage Sequence

The initial situation described by Rawls in which contractors choose principles of justice from behind a veil of ignorance identifies imperatives of the widest kind. For Rawls, democratic citizens acknowledge and recognize these principles as those that resonate with their self-conception and basic beliefs about the nature of society. We now turn from the analysis of the concept of justice to consider the practical import of the principles uncovered in the analysis. In the following five sections we will examine the move from principles of justice to the construction of a constitution, and the development of a legislative framework. Along the way we will consider three practical problems that Rawls uses to illustrate what the principles demand, both constitutionally and legislatively. These are the problems of toleration, political participation, and civil disobedience.

Rawls conceives of the contractors moving from the original position to a constitutional convention to which they would be delegates. This is the second stage of the sequence following the work done in the original position. The task of the constitutional convention is to write a constitution that is just by the terms of the principles of justice and that is suited to the requirements of a *particular* society. In other words, the delegates are required to give a practical expression to the principles of justice. They are primarily concerned with the "powers of government and the basic rights of citizens" (TJ: 172). In contrast to the contractors, the delegates look at how the first principle is to be realized in a particular constitution; they consider how to enshrine the liberties and rights of citizens. In order to achieve this they will have to know more about the particular circumstances of their society than they do under the veil of ignorance in the original position. Thus the veil is lifted but not entirely. The delegates know "the relevant general facts about their society, that is, its natural circumstances and resources, its level of economic advance and political culture, and so on" (TJ: 172–73). They do not know their own circumstances, their social and economic place in society, and the like. Therefore they cannot tailor the constitution for their own benefit, but they know enough to draft a constitution that benefits and is suited to their particular society. This suggests that the principles of justice are compatible with a range of possible of constitutions. What differs from one constitution to the next will be dictated by the social, political, and economic circumstances of the society to which the constitution is applied. Some basic rights will always be in place in any democratic society, such as freedom of conscience and the right to participate in the political process; however, other rights, such as a right to a free education, may depend on what resources are available to a society.

In the first instance, the task of the delegates is to write a constitution that maximizes the rights and liberties of all citizens in the context of their society. In the second instance, their task is to write a constitution that is an effective guide to the legislature. This latter consideration is important because the constitution provides the framework for the legislative process and thus also limits and restricts it. In summary, the delegates are charged with drafting a constitution that is just and effective. The standard for whether a constitution is just is set by the two principles agreed to in the original position.

The third stage of the sequence is the legislative stage. Delegates become legislators and are concerned with writing bills that govern social and economic policies. While attention in the second stage was on the first principle of justice (the greatest equal liberty principle), attention at the legislative stage is focused on the difference principle. The particular laws agreed to by the legislators must conform to the principles of justice and to the framework of the constitution. Rawls allows that the legislators will require more particular knowledge than the delegates to fashion bills appropriate to their society. Thus, the veil of ignorance is still further lifted in order that the work of drafting laws can proceed efficiently. Nonetheless, the legislators are kept ignorant of facts that will cause bias or prejudice in their judgments. In attending to social and economic questions legislators adopt the view of the least advantaged in society in accordance with the demands of the difference principle. For example, when setting out a program of taxes, they should consider how this program affects the welfare of those at the bottom of the economic ladder (assuming, as Rawls usually does, that such citizens are better off under an unequal distribution of resources than they would be under an equal distribution). Any advantages gained by the better off have to be compensated for by advantages to the worst off.

Lastly, the fourth stage of the sequence concerns "the application of rules to particular cases by judges and administrators, and the following of rules of citizens generally" (TJ: 175). At this stage the veil of ignorance is completely lifted and everyone has full knowledge of their particular circumstances. In a perfectly just society judges and administrators rule in accordance with just laws framed within the guidelines of a just constitution. This constitution is held to the standard of principles of justice chosen in an original position defined by its fairness. Rawls has moved from the very broadest question in the first stage (What is justice for democratic societies?) to the narrower question (What is a just constitution for a democratic society?) to an even narrower question (How should just laws be legislated?) to the narrowest of questions (How should judges and administrators apply the law?). He has argued that each stage is subordinated to the next and should be guided by the principles and rules articulated in the stage above it. Of course, this is an idealized description of how constitutions and laws are written and an idealization of how laws are applied to individual citizens. However, the stages are useful insofar as they offer us a definition of the role of constitutional conventions and legislatures from the perspective of questions of justice. They also define the relationship between these institutions when considering such questions. It also should be clear from this discussion that when Rawls talks of democracy he is referring to constitutional democracies, that is, democracies in which the constitution rather than legislature is sovereign.

CONSTITUTIONAL QUESTIONS

There are many constitutional questions facing delegates. One way to get at the kind of reasoning the delegates use in applying the two principles to these questions is to focus on particularly contentious and difficult issues. Thus, in the next few sections we turn our attention to the problem of toleration in a democratic society. Then we move on to the problem of guaranteeing effective political participation by citizens.

The Problem of Toleration

The problem of toleration has two parts. First, the delegates need to determine a constitutional principle that specifies when, if ever, the state may restrict liberty of conscience (or rather activities associated with, and expressions of, a citizen's conception of the good). Second, they need to consider what, if any, restrictions should apply to citizens whose conception of the good is itself intolerant. These problems arise, and indeed are particularly pressing, in democratic societies in which there is a plurality of conceptions of the good. In *A Theory of Justice* Rawls considers this problem in a narrow sense. But in his later work the consequences of this plurality of conceptions of the good in democratic societies will occupy much of this thought. At this juncture we are primarily concerned to explain how the delegates to the constitutional convention reason when considering the problem of toleration.

It is obvious that any state has to decide what it will tolerate. The state has a monopoly on coercive power. Therefore, it has the means to prevent actions and expressions of people whose ideas it wishes to silence. Furthermore in the ordinary course of events some actions and some expressions will threaten public security. The question facing the delegates is what counts as a threat to public security? The delegates are guided in their answer to this question by the reasoning of the contractors in the original position. The contractors treasure liberty above all else. The first principle enshrines this idea. Thus the first consideration the delegates attend to is how the first principle bears on the issue of toleration. *The test of toleration* will be the following: freedom of conscience (actions and expressions that follow from the exercise of this freedom) is to be restricted or denied only "to avoid an even greater injustice, an even greater loss of liberty" (TJ: 188).

From the point of the view of the contractors we can see how this test is arrived at. They do not know what their conception of the good is and so they have reason to be as liberal as possible in extending freedom of conscience. Although the delegates have more information they too are ignorant of their particular conception of the good and so they too will value freedom of conscience. Moreover the delegates recognize that their task of drafting a constitution is to be guided by the principles that emerge in the original position, and that the constitution is subordinate to these principles. A constitution in a democratic society will therefore allow any expression (understood very broadly) of opinion unless it is clearly shown that it infringes, restricts, or somehow abrogates some citizens' constitutionally protected freedoms. However, from the standpoint of citizens who are fully aware of their conception of the good the test will be challenging.

Many citizens regard their conception of the good as true. They not only regard their religious and metaphysical beliefs as correct, but also consider the religious and metaphysical beliefs of others as false. From the point of view of such citizens they are being asked (on the grounds of what was decided in the original position) to acquiesce in actions and expressions that they believe, and perhaps claim to "know," are false. There are deep philosophical difficulties lurking in the background. It might be claimed, for example, that someone who subordinated her religious convictions to the first principle of justice and consequently acquiesced to the test of toleration did not, after all, truly believe in her religion. Further, it might be asserted that acquiescing to the test demonstrates a general skepticism about truth claims concerning religion and metaphysics. Both of these claims suggest that Rawls's account of justice rubs up against people who regard their religious beliefs as paramount and who reject a general skepticism about values.

We will leave these concerns unaddressed for now because, as I mentioned earlier, these questions will come to occupy Rawls's attention in his later writings. What matters as this point is that Rawls demonstrates how a rule governing a controversial issue, like what the test for toleration should be in a democratic society, can be derived, at the constitutional stage, from an application of the greatest equal liberty principle. Rawls argues that (TJ: 188):

> Those who would deny liberty of conscience cannot justify their action by condemning philosophical skepticism and indifference to religion, not by appealing to social interests and affairs of the state. The limitation of liberty is justified only when it is necessary for liberty itself, to prevent an invasion of freedom that would be still worse.

The second part of the problem of toleration concerns the constitutional rule governing how the state should treat people with intolerant views. A citizen with an intolerant conception of the good makes a claim on the institutions of the state that they should restrict the actions and expressions of beliefs of other citizens on the grounds that other citizens hold false or immoral beliefs. In other words, intolerant people wish to impose their conception of the good on the rest. It might be tempting to argue that intolerant people do not deserve the protection of a constitution that would allow them the liberty of conscience to act, proclaim, and advocate their intolerance. However, from the point of view of the delegates to the constitutional convention, value judgments of this kind cannot be made since the delegates are unaware of their own particular values. Once again, the delegates turn to the principles established in the original position and the reasoning of the contractors. Therefore, the thinking that guides the constitutional rule the delegates agree to should not be surprising. Rawls puts it this way (TJ: 193): "The conclusion, then, is that while an intolerant sect does not itself have title to complain of intolerance, its freedom should be restricted only when the tolerant sincerely and with reason believe that their own security and that of the institutions of liberty are in danger." Citizens have claims against the institutions of the state only by appeal to two principles of justice. Therefore, the intolerant cannot demand that the state use its coercive power to impose a particular conception of the good on society as a whole because such a claim cannot be supported by the principles. The first principle is aimed at maximally extending, and not restricting, liberty, which the imposition of one sect's conception of the good will do. However, by the same reasoning, the rest of society may not restrict a particular conception of the good just because it advocates intolerance; merely advocating intolerance is not (necessarily) a restriction on anyone else's freedom. For example, let us assume my neighbor wants to impose a theocracy and holds meetings with others to promote this idea. My freedom is not abridged unless his actions succeed to the extent that my freedom is genuinely under threat. Rawls is concerned that restrictions placed on the intolerant should be based on a carefully considered, sincere, and well-founded belief that the institutions of the democratic state "are in danger." Thus merely disliking or being offended by my neighbor's beliefs is not grounds for calling in the police.

The main argument we can offer to those whose beliefs we restrict is that *they* would have chosen the principles of justice in the original position that are the source the restrictions they suffer. Thus, the challenge we offer them is the same one Rawls's analytic of justice offers the reader. If you accept the premises of the argument for the original position, and you agree with the reasoning of the contractors, then you also agree to the principles. Furthermore, if you agree to the principles and you also accept that the constitutional rules restricting freedom of conscience are properly founded on those principles, then you accept and agree to those restrictions *even if you are subject yourself to the restrictions.* This is a powerful challenge, which takes us back to the argument for imaginative identification. It is not a challenge that someone who rejects the premises of the original position will accept, of course. However, it invites the question of what we are committed to when accepting these premises and what will count as a tolerable conception of the good in a constitutional democracy. These questions we have to postpone for the moment and return to later in part two.

The Problem of Participation

The first principle prescribes the greatest extent of liberty for citizens compatible with other citizens' equal claim to liberty. From the perspective of the delegates to the constitutional convention this principle has to be applied to the political procedure. Therefore, constitutional rules need to be established that define political participation. Rawls specifically argues the delegates must consider the meaning and the extent of citizens' participation, as well as the measures that should be taken by the state to secure and enhance the "worth" of the political freedoms.

THE WORTH OF LIBERTY

The first problem of participation that Rawls addresses is how to ensure the *equal value* of the political liberties guaranteed by the first principle. Thus, we have to distinguish between having a right to something (participation, privacy, private property, and so on) and having the resources to make use of the right in question. Political justice demands that the constitution contain procedural rules that attend not just to the fact that citizens have constitutionally guaranteed rights but that citizens have "the fair value of political liberty" (TJ: 198). For Rawls, "those similarly endowed and motivated should have roughly the same chance of attaining positions of political authority irrespective of their economic and social class" (TJ: 197). The problem is that those with more resources can come to dominate the political process, thereby silencing the voices of the less resourced. What makes this a particularly acute problem is that no citizen has been denied her rights of political participation as such; she still has a constitutional right to participate based on the prescriptions of the first principle. However, the inequalities in resources and welfare that are allowed by the difference principle can have the effect of making her possession of that right worth less than the rights of others.

When reflecting on this problem the delegates adopt the perspective of the least advantaged in their society and consider to the lexical ordering of the principles of justice. The result of such considerations leads the delegates to draft rules that ensure that the effects of material inequalities are minimized. (Ideally they would be absent, but in practice the ideal is unlikely to be obtained.) In this framework, the least advantaged have a higher-order interest in realizing themselves as free and equal citizens and the priority of liberty is guaranteed by the lexical priority of the first principle. For example, Rawls argues that political parties should be publicly funded so that they are not bound to the agendas of special interest groups. The aim here is to make equal opportunities for political participation and thus guarantee equal citizenship safe from the effects of social and economic inequality.

Rawls's solution to the problem of the worth of liberty has not satisfied everyone. It relies on the effectiveness of the constitutional measures that would minimize the consequences of material inequality. However, there is another solution. Why would the contractors not simply disallow inequalities in resources and welfare and thereby guarantee the equal worth of the liberties? In fact, one could argue that if the contractors treasure their freedom and equality to the extent that Rawls insists they do, then would they not be very wary of allowing any diminishment of equal citizenship by the effects of social and economic inequalities? In short, would it not be *rational*, given their higher-order interests, for the contractors to collapse the first and second principle and demand equality across the board in rights, resources, and welfare?

This argument goes to the heart of Rawls's analytic of justice and clearly has dramatic consequences for the practical effects of his theory on societies. Rawlsian justice would demand a radical shift of resources and a massive alteration of the character of democratic societies. As we will see when we turn to Rawls's more detailed account of economic institutions in democratic societies, he will argue that his principles give rise to a "tendency to equality." This claim combined with his belief that the consequences of material inequalities between citizens can be sufficiently minimized might be enough to assuage the critic on this point. However, it is clear that there is a genuine tension between the first and second principles, a tension between the difference principle and the priority of liberty. We will return to these issues when we assess the objections to Rawls's theory.

Majority Rule

Another difficult issue for liberals has been the extent of democratic rule. Liberals have been wary of what Rawls calls "bare majority rule" where all decisions by the major institutions of society are dictated by the popular vote. Some would argue that this is simply what democracy is: rule by the people. However, Rawls joins the liberal tradition by arguing that majority rule should be constrained. The source of this constraint is the constitution which sets down rules that limit what "bare majorities" may achieve. The sorts of restrictions that Rawls has in mind are those like a bill of rights, a separation of powers between branches of government, or the requirement of a "super-majority" to change certain laws, and so on. In other words, Rawls offers an argument for a constitutional democracy against a popularist democracy.

The argument for these limitations is, once again, the argument from the priority of liberty. Thus, any restriction on popular democratic choice would have to be justified by the effect of such a restriction on the "system of liberty" as a whole. Therefore, the argument for constitutionalism would thus rest on a claim that constitutional constraints work to increase or maintain the most extensive system of liberty for all citizens. For example, it could be argued that a bill of rights, for example, protects the freedoms of individuals against the whims of majorities, and protects individuals from pressures to conform to group expectations. Rawls's point is that only these kinds of arguments will count when the delegates debate the extent of participation in the political process. For instance, they cannot argue that limitations on democratic participation are justified by economic gains since this would be a failure to acknowledge the priority of liberty. The point, once again, is that the delegates are always guided in their choices by the first principle and so it is in terms of this principle that constitutional constraints on the legislature can be justified.

LEGISLATIVE QUESTIONS

The third stage in Rawl's four-stage sequence is the reasoning of the representatives in the legislature. At this stage the legislators are concerned with drafting laws that govern the background conditions of social and economic activities. They are guided by the constitution and, ultimately, by the two principles. The legislators are primarily tasked with realizing the prescriptions of the difference principle. In order to be successful they need more information than the delegates or the contractors. They need to know many of the particulars of their society's economic situation in order to fashion the most just and efficient laws. The more detail we know, the less abstract our considerations will be. Thus Rawls does not offer specific recommendations. Instead he points out the *type* of reasoning the legislators engage in and the *kinds* of questions they consider. We examine the legislative problem of the social minimum below and the issues it raises concerning equality, self-respect, and the choice of economic system.

The Problem of the Social Minimum

The difference principle requires that inequalities in social and economic welfare be to the advantage of the worst off citizens. Differences in levels of welfare are measured by an index of primary goods. Those who are lowest on such an index must be better off than they would be on an equal distribution of primary goods. In order to achieve the prescriptions of the difference principle government must concern itself with the distribution of the primary goods and, indeed, with the transfer of primary goods from some citizens to others. Rawls's account of justice is therefore redistributive; it takes from some to give to others.

The difference principle offers only the most general guide for the legislators. On the surface it seems to require only that the worst-off be marginally better off than under an equal distribution, *no matter how well off the best-off are*. In other words, it could be argued that the difference principle sanctions limitless inequality between citizens justified on the grounds that the least-advantaged are fractionally advantaged by this unequal arrangement. This superficial reading would count as a considerable criticism if it could be supported. However, we should remember that the principles are not independent of one another. The constraints of the lexically prior greatest equal liberty principle act to diminish inequalities. Indeed, Rawls argues that the net effect of the two principles acting in concert is a "tendency to equality." Moreover, the primary good of self-respect also plays a role in constraining the extent of the inequalities between citizens. Thus, when the legislators consider the question of the level of the social minimum it is these constraints they attend to.

THE TENDENCY TO EQUALITY

The principles support an egalitarian conception of justice and oppose a meritocratic conception. The latter conception justifies an unequal distribution of welfare and resources on the grounds of desert. It argues that citizens who use their natural talents to acquire material primary goods deserve their advantages. A libertarian argument for a meritocracy goes further. It argues that not only do citizens deserve the advantages flowing from their natural talents but they have a right to the advantages that flow from the use of them. An alternative argument for a meritocracy is that rewarding people for usefully employing their natural talents is an efficient way to increase the overall welfare of society. Later we will look more closely at the libertarian criticisms of Rawls.

The first part of Rawls's response to these challenges is to say that we do *not* deserve our natural talents. They come to us via the "lottery of birth"; we have done nothing to deserve them. Therefore we do not deserve the advantages and disadvantages that result from the use of our natural talents. This "natural distribution" of talents is just a "natural fact." Thus, what matters for Rawls are the institutional arrangements that reward and cultivate some of these talents. The questions of justice apply to the institutional arrangements. It is easy to misunderstand Rawls and suppose he is allowing the state to have control over our bodies and what we do with them. This is not the case. A person's ability to play the piano or swing a baseball bat is *theirs*. For Rawls, these abilities are protected by the right to bodily integrity which falls under the greatest equal liberty principle. Rawls is not suggesting that citizens have no rights to their bodies or abilities. However, he is arguing that people have no natural right to profit from their piano playing or baseball talents. For Rawls (TJ: 87): "The difference principle represents, in effect, an agreement to regard the distribution of natural talents as in some respects a common asset and to share in the greater social and economic benefits made possible by the complementariness of this distribution." And further (TJ: 87): "The naturally advantaged are not to gain merely because they are more gifted, but only to cover the costs of training and education and for using their endowment in ways that help the less fortunate as well."

It is in this sense that the best-off citizens do not deserve their natural assets. In fact, the language of desert is inappropriate because it asks the wrong question from the wrong point of view. When considering questions of justice Rawls demands that we adopt the "general point of view" or "Archimedean point." This perspective makes it clear that our possession of natural assets is contingent and arbitrary, and consequently irrelevant when deciding on a just distribution of primary goods. Further, it is a contingent matter whether the kind of society we are born into rewards the kinds of talents we have. This is an additional reason to agree with Rawls. Moreover, the general point of view allows the best-off to recognize that their advantages are the result of a joint cooperative enterprise with their fellow citizens and so the interests and welfare of others are not alien but bound up with their own.

Rawls therefore argues that a meritocratic conception misconstrues the requirements of just distribution. First, it fails to distinguish between the possession of natural talents and being entitled to benefit from them. Second, it fails to recognize the cooperative nature of society. Thus, it fails to recognize the connectedness of citizens and their welfare. An egalitarian conception of justice, of which the difference principle is a part, makes the right kinds of distinctions and acknowledges that society is a cooperative venture in which the fate of *all* citizens is decided.

A further argument for a meritocracy is made on the basis of its *efficiency*. An economic system is efficient if one can make a person better off only by making some other person worse off. At this stage we need not discuss the many technical issues underlying the application of a principle of efficiency to an economic system. Suffice to say that an economic system has many distributions that are efficient. A meritocracy may be efficient in its distribution of resources. However, as Rawls says, the difference principle also yields an efficient distribution. What distinguishes them is not so much the question of efficiency but rather different theories of justice. The Rawlsian theory seeks the efficient distribution that marries the lexically prior requirements of the greatest equal liberty principle with the difference principle. Thus, even if an economic system governed by meritocratic principles yielded greater economic resources overall, Rawlsians would not sacrifice political liberties and personal freedoms in exchange for greater material welfare. A just distribution is an efficient one, but not all efficient distributions are just.

If we pool the value of natural assets, acknowledge the reciprocal nature of society, apply the difference principle with its requirements to better the position of the least-advantaged, and ensure equal opportunity, what are the practical consequences? Rawls provides the following example (TJ: 86): "In pursuit of this principle greater resources might be spent on the education of the less rather than the more intelligent, at least over a certain time of life, say the earlier years of school." The contractors view the future always as if they were the least advantaged person in society. The original position is set up so that it is rational to do so. What matters if one is among the least intelligent in society is one's capacity to participate fully as a citizen in society. The resources required to live a full life as free and equal citizens may be greater for such persons than for the more naturally gifted. Of course, it will be important to develop the talents of the gifted too because it is their talents that will be most productive later in life. The imperative is to equalize opportunity so as to overcome arbitrary and contingent factors (including natural endowments of intelligence) as far as this is possible. Where such endowments do result in advantage for some citizens the imperative is ensure that the worst-off also benefit from this advantage.

It is easy to imagine how resources in a just society would be distributed to compensate for natural and class differences and how, where such differences persist, resources would be transferred to the worse-off. In short, there is a "tendency to equality" in a just Rawlsian society. Thus, differences in material welfare should not be very great given the distributive requirements of the difference principle and the constraints of the greatest equal liberty principle.

Self-Respect

The second major consideration for the legislators when debating the social minimum is the role of the primary good of self-respect. For Rawls (TJ: 156):

> by arranging inequalities for reciprocal advantage and by abstaining from the exploitation of the contingencies of nature and social circumstance within a framework of equal liberties, persons express their respect for one another in the very constitution of their society. In this way they insure their self-respect as it is rational for them to do.

Self-respect has two features for Rawls. First, it is a sense that a person has of their own value and worth. This arises from her sense that her conception of the good and the life plan founded on it are worthwhile. Second, self-respect supposes a measure of confidence in one's capacity to carry out one's plan of life. We need to emphasize that Rawls does not mean that justice requires that citizens are in possession of a particular *psychological attitude*. Justice, as Rawls has often enough said, concerns institutions and the way these institutions distribute rights, liberties, and welfare. The subjective psychological states of citizens are not the direct concern of institutions. However, the importance of self-respect as an attitude and the essential confidence of citizens to carry forward their plans of life, entails that just institutions do have an interest in providing the institutional platform so that citizens can develop and sustain self-respect. Rawls also thinks that self-respect is essential in a just society because it is from this that the possibility of respect for others emerges. The centrality that Rawls gives to respect reflects the Kantian intuitions that underpin much of the thinking in *A Theory of Justice.* Indeed, Rawls uses Kant's famous dictum to emphasize that respect requires us to treat people as ends in themselves and not as merely a means to our own ends.

The good of self-respect is one that emerges from the successful functioning of the two principles. Being secure in one's rights and liberties, and being a member of a cooperative scheme from which one draws one's just share, are bases for the development and maintenance of a sense of one's own worth. Furthermore, it is precisely these rights, liberties, income, and wealth that provide the means for pursuing and realizing one's conception of the good. The two principles, functioning in accord with one another, serve to *publicly affirm* a citizens' place in the social order, and thereby provide the basis for self-respect.

The legislators, therefore, need to consider self-respect when setting the social minimum. Rawls's argument that self-respect is the most important of the primary goods means that the legislators would have to give priority to the question of whether the least-advantaged in society had the means to acquire and sustain their sense of self-worth. All citizens have an equal share of basic rights and the political liberties. Furthermore, in accordance with the difference principle, we know that the least-advantaged are better off than under an equal distribution. However, once we realize that the state is required to secure the institutional bases of self-respect we will see that the social minimum will be set high enough to eliminate or greatly diminish actual inequalities and differences between citizens. In evaluating the criticism we considered earlier that the difference principle allows for very great inequalities between citizens, we can now see that this is a superficial reading of Rawls's account of justice. It is superficial because it reads the principles independently of each other and it fails to consider the emergent effects of the principles working together. Adding these considerations together shows how the actual inequalities between citizens in a just Rawlsian society will be quite minimal.

This defense of Rawls will not satisfy everyone. Indeed, it will certainly not satisfy the libertarian. Thus, we will examine further libertarian criticisms of Rawls's account of justice later. However, for our present expository purposes we can now understand more clearly how Rawls's principles work together.

Choice of Economic Regime

Among the basic institutions that realize the two principles is the economic regime. The choice between economic regimes is made on the grounds of which regime is capable of instantiating the norms and requirements of the justice principles. Rawls argues that there are two such regimes that meet these requirements; in the process he rejects three others. The five candidate economic systems are the following: laissez-faire capitalism, welfare-state capitalism, state socialism, a property-owning democracy, and democratic socialism. Rawls rejects laissez-faire capitalism because it "secures only formal equality and rejects the fair value of equal political liberties and fair equality of opportunity" (JF: 137). In other words, it lacks mechanisms for preventing the uncontrolled accumulation of material primary goods. When this happens political power becomes vested in the hands of the few, making the liberties enshrined in the first principle merely formal rather than actual. Mechanisms of distribution and redistribution, or "background conditions" as Rawls calls them, are therefore required to ensure that citizens have equality of opportunity in a substantive rather than merely in a formal sense.

Rawls also rejects welfare-state capitalism. This is not clear from his arguments in *A Theory of Justice*. The argument against welfare-state capitalism is only made much later in his 2001 book, *Justice as Fairness: A Restatement*. On the surface it would seem that such an economic regime would be a genuine candidate for a just society. However, Rawls argues that even where welfare grants are generous such a regime also fails to support substantive political equality and equality of opportunity. It permits entrenched and large inequalities in wealth and income ameliorated by payments to the worst-off. This leads to the possibility of a large and *permanent* underclass of citizens emerging. Once again, the problem is that under such a regime actual political power is likely to be in the hands of the few. Thus it would be a democracy only in a formal sense. The rejection of both these candidates shows that what matters to Rawls is that an economic system is subservient to the requirements of the first principle of justice. This is to be expected given the reasoning of the contractors in the original position and such reasoning will be reflected in the reasoning of the legislators.

The third candidate economic regime is state socialism which Rawls quickly rejects. State socialism organizes economic activity through a state bureaucracy "supervised by a one party regime" (JF: 138). Thus, state socialism fails the test of democracy simply because it denies equal rights of political participation and freedom of conscience.

The final two options, a property-owning democracy and democratic socialism both satisfy the norms and requirements of the two principles. The main difference between the two regimes is that the former allows for private ownership of the means of production (or "productive assets"), whereas in the latter workers directly or indirectly own and control the means of production. Private ownership of personal property is guaranteed as a right under the first principle. The question of whether private or public ownership of the means of production should prevail depends on "circumstances, institutions and historical conditions" (TJ: 248). In other words, it is a legislative question. Both regimes satisfy the two principles because they support both the "fair value" of the political liberties and equality of opportunity. They achieve this through the setting up of background conditions and primarily tax mechanisms that ensure a wide distribution of ownership of capital and land. Rawls writes (TJ: 247):

> The taxation of inheritance and income at progressive rates (when necessary), and the legal definition of property rights, are to secure the institutions of equal liberty in a property-owning democracy and the fair value of the rights they establish. Proportional expenditure (or income taxes) are to provide revenue for public goods, the transfer branch and the establishment of fair equality of opportunity in education, and the like, so as to carry out the second principle.

Both a property-owning democracy and democratic socialism rely on markets to regulate price and distribution of goods and services. They both also allow for redistribution and thus the regulation of markets. The motive that underlies the regulation of markets is to make political liberties and rights meaningful. Since both regimes subordinate the market to this ideal they are therefore both capable of instantiating the two principles.

Rawls discusses democratic socialism very briefly and clearly regards a property-owning democracy, which permits the private ownership of productive assets, as the main candidate for an economic regime in a just or nearly just regime. This is not surprising given the traditions of modern Western democracies whose citizens are the main audience for Rawls's argument. If there is no principled reason for preferring one over the other then the choice can only be made on the basis of the particularities and circumstances of the society that the legislators work within. Opponents of Rawls will, of course, complain on both ends of the argument. Libertarians take property rights in general to be fundamental to the requirements of justice and reject the idea that property is something to be distributed and redistributed by the state. They oppose Rawls's ideal of a property-owning democracy and favor laissez-faire capitalism. Radical socialists will reject Rawls's idea that democratic socialism is compatible with market mechanisms for the distribution of goods and services. For them markets are the cause of alienation and exploitation of workers.

In conclusion, the practical questions facing the legislators in the third stage of the four-stage sequence are those concerning the distribution of social and economic resources. One very important question they face is how to determine the social minimum. Philosophy cannot prescribe, in the abstract, what this should be since it depends on the circumstances of the society in question. However, we have been able to point out the sorts of reasons that will have the greatest weight for the legislators when they finally determine what the social minimum should be for their society.

ADMINISTRATIVE QUESTIONS

The final stage of the four-stage sequence concerns the application of the laws to individual citizens by administrators and judges. At this stage when all the facts about citizens' particular circumstances are known, the veil of ignorance is completely lifted. Administrators and judges are interpreters of the laws and, sometimes, the constitutional principles embodied in the laws, which are, in turn, derived from the principles arrived at in the original position. The interpretive function of judges and administrators brings to the surface a feature of the four-stage sequence that has not yet been emphasized. The original position is an example of *perfect* procedural justice in which the outcome defines justice *whatever* that outcome is. Therefore, in the case of the original position there is not an external standard against which we can measure the justness of the principles adopted by the contractors; as long as the procedure is sound then the principles that emerge from the procedure are defining of justice. However, the constitutional stage and the legislative stage are examples of *imperfect* procedural justice. First, there is an external standard that counts as a measure of the justice of the constitutional rules and the legislators bills; namely the two principles. Second, there is no procedure that will guarantee that the rules and bills adopted best meet the standard of justice prescribed by the two principles. This is partly because the delegates and legislators are forced to attempt to marry the principles to their political, social, and economic circumstances, and this requires judgment and speculation. Furthermore, for any particular society, there are a number of possible of constitutions that are genuine candidates for efficiently and effectively realizing the two principles. Consequently, citizens can, with good will, disagree with the rules and laws adopted in their society and argue that some are unjust. Some rules fail to meet the standards set by the two principles. Therefore, some citizens may have laws applied to them by judges and administrators that they sincerely believe to be unjust. The practical concern at this stage then is not with how the administrators and judges reason, since they apply the results of the reasoning of the delegates and legislators, but rather the reasoning of citizens who sincerely believe that unjust laws are being applied to them. This practical concern raises a set of questions about citizens' obligations and duties and what justice demands of them. So far we have been primarily concerned with how the principles of justice apply to institutions whereas here we are concerned with the obligations of individuals to those institutions.

The Problem of Civil Disobedience

Rawls argues that citizens in a just, or a nearly just, society have a duty to comply with unjust laws under most circumstances. Disagreement between citizens about particular rules and laws will arise. However, provided the background conditions of a society are just or nearly just, then citizens should not take these sorts of disagreements as grounds for noncompliance. We would expect such citizens to use their political liberties to persuade their fellow citizens to change what they perceive to be unjust laws. Nevertheless, as Rawls points out (TJ: 308):

> The injustice of a law is not, in general, a sufficient reason for not adhering to it any more than the legal validity of legislation (as defined by the existing constitution) is sufficient reason for going along with it. When the basic structure of society is reasonably just, as estimated by what the current state of things allows, we are to recognize unjust laws as binding provided that they do not exceed certain limits of injustice.

Of course, if a society is unjust in the larger sense of failing to meet the basic requirements of the principles of justice, for example, where basic liberties and rights are denied, where opportunities are reserved for the few, and subjects are economically exploited, then compliance with the laws of such an unjust regime is not expected. Whether one has duty to resist such a regime and at what cost to oneself is a question left unanswered. Thus, there is a general duty of compliance with laws in a just or nearly just society. However, the very idea of civil disobedience suggests a conflict between the duty just mentioned and another duty to challenge or resist unjust laws, even in nearly just societies. This presents a conflict between a duty of compliance and a further duty of enlarging and maintaining justice.

What is civil disobedience? Rawls defines it in the following way (TJ: 320): "a public, non-violent, conscientious yet political act contrary to law usually done with the aim of bringing about a change in the law or policies of the government." A genuine act of civil disobedience is a political act in two ways. First, it is aimed at changing the law, and second, it is not guided by sectarian interests. This second condition rules out as acts of civil disobedience those that are grounded in religious or cultural doctrines, that is, acts which aim at furthering a partial agenda. An act of civil disobedience must therefore appeal to general principles for its justification (that is, the principles of justice) and not a particular conception of the good. It is a dramatic appeal to what are believed to be common conceptions of justice. Its purpose is to show that some existing law fails the standard set by that common conception of justice. Furthermore, an act of civil disobedience is contrary to the law but at the same time faithful to the law. A demonstrator breaks the law by her act of disobedience but accepts and expects to be punished for breaking the law. There is therefore, paradoxically, an expression of fidelity to the law in the act of breaking it. After all, the demonstrator seeks only a change in the law; she wishes the law to be obeyed as a general principle. Finally, acts of civil disobedience are nonviolent. They aim at persuasion by appeal to reasons that could be accepted by all citizens. Violence offers reasons of a kind, but not the sort of reasons that result in the willing acceptance of an alternative point of view. The point is not to violate the basic rights and liberties of fellow citizens, but rather protect and where necessary extend them.

This is what Rawls understands as a genuine act of civil disobedience. The next issue to consider is when acts of this sort are justified. The first condition Rawls sets out is that the law objected to must result in a "substantial and clear" injustice. The less disagreement there is about the fact of an injustice the better the case for civil disobedience, and the more likely it is that the act will result in a change in the law. He goes on to say (TJ: 326): "there is a presumption in favor of restricting acts of civil disobedience to serious infringements of the first principle of justice, the principle of equal liberty, and to blatant violations of the second part of the second principle, the principle of fair equality of opportunity." The claim is that violations of the requirements of the greatest equal liberty principle are more obvious and, importantly, more urgent (given its lexical priority). Violations are also often obvious when citizens are denied rights of equal opportunity. However, Rawls thinks that the application of the difference principle is less easy to classify as unjust, in part because this involves "theoretical and speculative" beliefs. Though the more clear the violation and the more substantially it affects the liberties and rights of citizens the greater the justification for acts of civil disobedience. The second condition Rawls sets out is that citizens who engage in acts of civil disobedience do so as a last resort. This condition supposes that they have first made political appeals "in good faith" but have been rebuffed by legislators. The third condition for the justification of acts of civil disobedience is that they do not substantially threaten or substantially disrupt the "nearly just" constitution. The scenario that Rawls imagines is a number of groups in society all with grievances that meet the first two conditions laid out above but who, *if they acted at the same time*, would collectively pose a threat to the social order by their disobedience. Of course, if the society is manifestly unjust, this may be warranted. However, Rawls's assumption throughout his discussion is of a "nearly just" society. Thus, there is good reason why citizens should maintain such a society and not substantially threaten it, even if their particular grievance is justified.

These are the three conditions that would justify an act of civil disobedience. There is one further justification that that Rawls considers. He asks whether and why the contractors in the original position would permit such acts. He argues that they would allow for such acts for two main reasons. First, they would recognize that injustices can occur in nearly just societies (presumably, this is what makes them "nearly" just). Therefore, to deny citizens the opportunity to make a genuine and purposeful challenge to such injustices would be disrespectful by either making citizens acquiesce, inviting contempt, or making them resist the law. This could cause a division in society and a failure of mutual respect. A second reason that the contractors would allow for civil disobedience is that such acts can have the effect, over time, of making the liberties that the contractors treasure more secure. Rawls says (TJ: 337): "Although this mode of action is strictly speaking contrary to law, it is nevertheless a morally correct way of maintaining a constitutional regime." The security and protection of liberties always trumps other considerations for the contractors and so this is the most powerful of arguments for the legitimacy of acts of civil disobedience. However, we should not forget that this reasoning is in tension with another consideration that the contractors take very seriously, namely, the presumption that, in a well-ordered society, citizens comply with the law. It would be irrational to enter into an agreement that one believed that others will not abide by. And so the presumption of compliance is also a deep rational principle dear to the contractors.

The problem of civil disobedience illustrates the practical challenges of the fourth stage where we are concerned with duties of individual citizens to both the institutions of society and to one another.

We now have the two main elements of Rawls's theory of justice as fairness in place: the analytic of justice that provides an account of what the principles of justice are and how they are arrived at, and the practicum of justice that explains how the principles are applied in the circumstances of particular societies. We now have to step back and look more closely at the theoretical basis of the arguments that underlie Rawls's theory.

4. The Theoretical Basis of Justice

We have examined the argument leading to the two principles in the analytic of justice and taken a wider and more detailed view of these principles and their practical consequences for some of the urgent problems any theory of justice confronts. It is time to investigate more closely three of the main theoretical bases of his theory. Broadly speaking, we can divide these bases into the following categories: First, we examine the account of justification Rawls offers by looking at the ideas of "reflective equilibrium" and "procedural justice"; second, we examine what Rawls calls the "Aristotelian Principle," which is used to explain the deeper motivational assumptions that lie behind the theory of justice as fairness; and finally, we look at the most fundamental of Rawls's arguments, namely, the claim that right takes priority over the good.

Justification of the Principles

The question of what justifies the two principles has, in one sense, already been answered. The principles are justified because they would be chosen and agreed to by the contractors in a suitably defined initial situation. The analytic of justice defined the initial situation and showed, in a deductive fashion, why the contractors would agree to the two principles Rawls proposes. However, there are some obvious questions to be asked about this account of justification. For instance, why is *agreement* the basis of justification? Surely, we can agree to *anything*, and so merely agreeing to the principles cannot justify them in the sense Rawls demands. Moreover, should we not demand that the principles that govern the basic institutions of society be *true*? Is truth not the strongest form of justification we can have, and if so why settle for a mere agreement? These questions engage very deep epistemological issues in moral and political theory. Rawls's response to these issues in *A Theory of Justice* is an account of justification he calls reflective equilibrium.

REFLECTIVE EQUILIBRIUM—NARROW AND WIDE

We can begin by distinguishing two ways to think about the justification of our judgments in general. The first way is to suppose that our judgments are justified because they correspond to some external, independent realm of fact. Such a realm makes our judgments true when they correspond and false when they do not. To assume that our political and moral judgments require this sort of justification is to take a position we can call "foundationalist." The second way is to suppose that our judgments are justified when they cohere, that is, when our intuitions, our considered reflections, and the facts as we understand them all stand together in a harmonious structure. Rawls rejects the first account of justification as a flawed account of the epistemology of values. Instead he adopts the coherence account of justification. Thus, Rawls opts for a nonfoundationalist account of political values.

We can build the argument for the coherentist approach to justification in stages. First, principles of justice cannot be whatever we happen to want them to be. If our judgments about justice were entirely subjective (like our judgments about taste), then there would be no point in constructing a normative theory of justice. Instead, we could make do with a psychology of people's justice preferences. Insofar as we are concerned to say how society's basic institutions *ought* to be arranged we must leave behind preferences that are entirely subjective. However, there is also something very wrong in thinking that what justice is could be entirely disconnected from our intuitions. For example, as Rawls argues, a just society could not be one that permitted "religious intolerance and racial discrimination." We are highly confident that such societies are fundamentally unjust. We would think a theory of justice that advocated intolerance and discrimination had got justice wrong. Thus, while a theory of justice cannot be entirely subjective, it also cannot be entirely removed from what we think justice is supposed to be. The challenge becomes one of finding a sense of objectivity suited to the problem of justice, a sense that navigates between the subjective constraints on what justice can be and the objective demands for justification.

The idea of reflective equilibrium is Rawls's answer to this challenge. In approaching the problem of what justice demands he asks us to begin with our "considered convictions of justice" (TJ: 18). An example of such a conviction would be our confidence that racial discrimination is unjust. However, this is not a mere conviction but it is one that we have reflected on and "considered," that is, subjected to philosophical scrutiny. Part of such consideration will also be testing our judgments against our knowledge of the world. For instance, racial discrimination not only rests on philosophically dubious claims about the moral inequality of some persons, but it also rests on false factual claims about such persons regarding their intelligence, and so on. Thus we need to move from philosophical reflection and empirical investigation concerning our judgments towards principles that capture these considered judgments in an imperative form. These principles then serve as guides—practical guides to how our institutions are to be arranged and political guides for making judgments about the justice of such institutions.

We would expect that the process of reflection will make us reconsider some of our convictions, perhaps changing our understanding of them and what they entail and, occasionally, causing us to abandon a conviction entirely. Once we arrive at principles of justice we then test them in turn against our now reconsidered convictions. Our aim is to arrive at a coherence and harmony between our convictions and the principles that guide us. When we achieve such coherence we have arrived at a point of *narrow* reflective equilibrium. It is narrow at this point because what we have achieved is a coherence and order in the way we think about questions of justice. We have, as it were, tidied up our values and become reflective about the principles that underlie them.

Narrow reflective equilibrium is contrasted to *wide* reflective equilibrium. This is achieved when we test our considered convictions and our principles against alternative accounts of what justice requires. These alternative accounts come to us from what Rawls describes as the "philosophical tradition." It is against this tradition that we compare and consider our own understanding of justice. What is important is not that we have contrasted our view with some possible others (other views that we might have imagined), but that we have contrasted it with the systematic theories that have stood the test of time in our intellectual tradition. In this way we step even further from our subjective prereflective opinions about justice and move from mere coherence (narrow reflective equilibrium) to an engagement with the ideas of others (wide reflective equilibrium). The kinds of theories Rawls has in mind are accounts of justice like utilitarianism. This is why it is important not only to lay out an argument for the two principles but also to show why these principles are superior to their alternatives.

We can think of this process as one that lays bare our sense of justice as a whole. It reveals our convictions, our capacity for reflection, and the organizing principles that, ideally, make our ideas about justice cohere. Rawls, at one point, describes the process as similar to revealing the grammatical structure of a language (TJ: 41). In the way the grammar of a language is, in some sense, hidden and needs to be brought to the surface the structure of our sense of justice is likewise hidden and needs to be revealed. This is why Rawls describes justice as fairness as "a theory of our moral sentiments" (TJ: 104).

The idea of reflective equilibrium is an ideal because philosophical reflection does not come to an end and the world throws up new facts. Ideally, we would lay out all our convictions, subject them to an exhaustive philosophical analysis, have all the facts on hand, and also have available all possible permutations of principles of justice from the philosophical tradition. No such ideal is realizable, of course. However, this is not to say that our judgments concerning justice are therefore unjustified because the ideal is unreachable. Justification in political theory, for Rawls, is a matter of degrees; we can be more or less justified in our judgments. The more our judgments are in reflective equilibrium the more justified our principles of justice are. What this denies is the tempting thought that closure is possible on these kinds of questions. We can never say, definitively, that this or that set of institutions is just. The most we can say is that we have good reason to think that they are just. However, on the other end of the scale we can be more certain about what we judge to be unjust regimes. But even here we have to allow that closure is not possible.

It should be obvious now that the analytic of justice is an attempt to arrive at a point of reflective equilibrium. We can think of the original position as a way of setting out our considered convictions concerning our self-conception (who we are and what motivates us) and as a representation of reasoning towards coherence in our ideas about justice in the light of alternatives. The constraints in the original position such as the veil of ignorance are simply a means of curbing our subjective tendencies and thus they push us forward towards a more objective, and therefore more justifiable, point of view. Insofar as we follow Rawls on this journey, that is, allow ourselves to imaginatively identify with the contractors and take their reasoning as our own, we, too, arrive at a place of wide reflective equilibrium. The original position is thus a device for achieving this.

Rawls's account of justification invites a number of important questions. I want to briefly raise two of them here. First, who is the "we" in this account of justification? Second, is this account of justification sufficient to deliver what it promises? In one sense the "we" are you and me, the readers of Rawls's *A Theory of Justice*. It is we who are asked by the text to imaginatively identify with the contractors and who are guided towards wide reflective equilibrium. However, as we have repeatedly seen, what Rawls has in mind is that the thinking of the contractors, placed as they are within the constraints of the original position, represents the fundamental intuitions of citizens in a society with a history of democratic institutions. The analytic of justice is thus an excavation of these intuitions and a deep philosophical reflection on them in the context of an intellectual tradition common to democratic societies. Now, it should be clear from this that the idea of reflective equilibrium is both a general account of justification and, in the hands of Rawls, an argument for the justification of principles of justice for democratic societies.

We can imagine that citizens of nondemocratic societies could arrive a point of wide reflective equilibrium about justice that would be very different from our own. In short, we must be careful to distinguish the method from the application of the method to a particular case. This distinction leads us though to question the assumption that citizens in a democratic society have a set of shared convictions. What grounds do we have to assume such a claim? If the claim is false, then the theory is in trouble. Then, even within democratic societies, there will be as many justified accounts of the justice of the basic institutions as there are sets of convictions. As we will see in part two, Rawls will describe this as the problem of pluralism in democratic societies. His answer to this problem is a theory of *political* liberalism, which we will examine in detail in part two.

The second question asked above cannot be fully answered at this stage. We will have to wait until we examine Rawls's account of political liberalism for the complete answer. However, we can register a worry about the idea of reflective equilibrium as it is used in *A Theory of Justice*. Some readers will not be convinced that the account of justification it offers is strong enough. They will argue that being in agreement with oneself (having a considered and coherent set of convictions and principles—narrow reflective equilibrium) and being satisfied that this coherence meets the test of the philosophical tradition (wide reflective equilibrium) lacks an important requirement of justification. Namely, that there is, in principle, general agreement on the reasons that count towards the justification. The thought here is that it is not enough that you or I are satisfied with the reasons we have for holding a point of view, but that we can, in principle at least, persuade others of our point of view as well. In other words, the kinds of reasons we have must be such that they will appeal to others too. We have to go beyond ourselves and cast our reasoning in a form that others can, in principle, acknowledge and take as their own reasons. Therefore, it is not yet sufficient for us to achieve narrow and wide reflective equilibrium, we have to take a further step and offer what Rawls will call *public reasons*, that is, reasons that other citizens *could* accept as their own. Where such reasons are accepted as settled we will have achieved a third and final stage of reflective equilibrium—*general* or *full* reflective equilibrium. We will continue our discussion of public reasons and full reflective equilibrium in part two.

For now, though, we can summarize Rawls's account of justification by saying that he offers a coherentist and nonfoundationalist theory of justification. The doctrine of reflective equilibrium seeks coherence among our intuitions, beliefs and principles. Further, Rawls argues that this coherence is not reflective of, nor does it in any way track, a "realm of moral fact." Thus, it is a nonfoundationalist account of justice that aims at wide reflective equilibrium.

The Right and the Good

Sometimes the right and the good conflict; it might be right to obey a principle even though the good of the persons involved is not preserved or advanced by obeying it. Conversely, the good of some persons may be maintained or advanced but only by doing what a principle forbids. A theory of justice has to determine an order of priority between the right and the good to settle these conflicts. Justice as fairness gives priority to the right and thus subordinates the good to the right. Utilitarianism, by contrast, subordinates the right to the good, specifying that the maximization of the good (happiness, the satisfaction of desire, or utility) trumps the constraints of principle. However, the relation of the right to the good is more complicated than this suggests. We need to gain an understanding of what Rawls means by saying that justice as fairness gives priority to the right over the good.

The purpose of the original position is to arrive at principles of right, which are principles of justice that ought to govern the basic institutions of a democratic society. As we have seen, these principles are derived from a statement about the nature of the contractors and their method of reasoning. The contractors are denied knowledge of their conception of the good (although they know that they have one) and so no substantive, or thick, notion of the good plays a part in the derivation of the principles. Thus, the contractors cannot tailor principles to suit their idea of the good (their moral, religious, or metaphysical beliefs). This is one way to ensure that the principles of right are not a substantive notion of the good in disguise. However, as we have seen, the contractors need something to work with when they decide between competing candidate principles of justice; they have to have something to deliberate *about*. At this juncture Rawls introduces the primary goods so that they can adjudicate between sets of principles by determining, in a broad way, how various principles of justice distribute primary goods among citizens in well-ordered societies. Now, clearly, primary goods are *goods* and so they reflect some idea of the good. Rawls says that they are goods that are essential for any citizen to advance her particular conception of the good. He describes them as part of a thin (rather than thick) theory of the good. Therefore, we require two explanations from Rawls: the first to explain precisely in what way the right constrains the good, the second to offer a justification for the thin theory of the good that is essential to the derivation of the principles of justice in the original position. We will begin with the second of these explanations.

THE THIN THEORY OF THE GOOD AND THE ARISTOTELIAN PRINCIPLE

A theory of the good says that something is good for someone or some collection of people. Therefore, what is good is also to say, or at least imply, something about the people for whom this is a good. This means that inevitably, we are forced into offering a theory of persons, their motivations and inclinations, along with an account of the good. Thus, if the primary goods constitute the basic necessities for developing and advancing a thick conception of the good, then we will have to say what it is about people that make these goods necessary goods for them. As we will see below, the Aristotelian principle is Rawls's answer to this question about the nature of persons.

However, before setting out the Aristotelian principle we should spell out Rawls's thin account of the good. We begin with basic idea of "goodness as rationality." For reasons we discuss later it is rational to want what is good. What Rawls means by rationality is fairly straightforward. First, in a situation of choice it is rational to select the most *effective* means to achieving the end desired. Second, it is rational to be *inclusive* in one's choice. This means that given two options, A and B, if B effectively achieves all the ends A achieves plus some further ends a person has reason to achieve, then it is rational to choose B over A. Finally, it is rational to make that choice of end that has the *most likelihood* of being achieved. If this is what is meant by rationality, what then is meant by good? To say that something is good is to say that it has properties (to a higher degree) it is rational to want in a thing of that kind. For example, a car is a good car if it has certain desirable properties (like an efficient engine, safe road holding, fuel efficiency, and so on) to a greater degree than other cars. Since I want a good car and a Subaru instantiates the properties of a good car, then it is rational for me to want a Subaru. This is a good car *for me*. However, if fuel efficiency is not a desirable property for you then this might not be a good car for you. We could go on to say that having a car of this kind fits with my plan of life; my plan incorporates the use of a reliable, fuel efficient, and safe car. Furthermore, it could still be a good car, in that it has properties I want in a car, but not be good for me because it failed to fit my plan of life. For instance, I have a strong belief that cars damage the environment and this belief trumps my desire for efficient transport. Thus, taking into account the priority I give to my beliefs about the environment, owning a Subaru would not fit into a fully rational plan of life for me even though a Subaru is a good car and such a car would effectively satisfy my desire for reliable transport.

Thus, the very definition of what is good makes use of the idea of rationality; it is rational to want what is good since good things are effective means to satisfying our ends. Concealed in this formulation is a particular view of the fundamental nature of persons. For Rawls, people have "plans of life"; they are deliberative and end-oriented creatures. To live a properly human life is to set about achieving some set of ends. Moreover, we understand one another in terms of our plans of life. When we ask a simple question like "What does that person want?" we presuppose a sense of what is good and a plan to search for the means to get what that person takes to be good. We should not be misled by the word "plan" and think that Rawls assumes we all have detailed, fully transparent, fully consistent sets of personal goals. Most of us clearly do not.

However, we all do have some kind of direction in life, some more or less cogent set of aims, some long-term ends (even if the plan is to "go with the flow"). Ideally our plan of life is rational since such a plan would be a good plan to have. It would be effective, inclusive (the best among alternative plans available to us), and the most likely to be achieved. Thereby, it would have the properties of a plan of life to the highest degree that one would rationally want in a plan of life.

From these considerations we can now turn to the question of what counts as a rational plan of life for a person. Rawls's answer is again fairly straightforward. A rational life plan is the plan that a person would choose with full "deliberative rationality." By this latter phrase, Rawls means a plan chosen with full information. This plan includes all the relevant facts, the consequences of a person's choices, chosen from the largest set of possible plans, etc. For Rawls (TJ: 366): "The best plan for an individual is the one that he would adopt if he possessed full information. It is the objectively rational plan for him and determines his real good." We are never in the position of having full information and so we are never fully deliberatively rational. Thus, we cannot determine in any final sense what counts as an objectively rational plan of life for ourselves and what our real good is. However, we can achieve partial deliberative rationality and seek a more rather than a less objectively rational plan of life for ourselves.

Rawls has argued that people have plans of life that are more or less rational and that persons seek their good through enacting their plans of life. The next step appears small but is crucial to the overall argument. Rawls now argues that we are *motivated* to realize our plans. In some ways this step is embedded in the definition of rationality. We seek, or are motivated, to realize our ends effectively. However, Rawls wants to go further and argue that we are motivated not only to realize our plans but that we "enjoy" increasingly complex activities associated with our capacities. Thus, we are motivated to seek more elaborate plans and the greater use of complex skills and capacities. This is the Aristotelian principle, which he describes as "deep psychological fact" (TJ: 379) about us. For Rawls (TJ: 374): "other things being equal, human beings enjoy the exercise of their realized capacities (their innate or trained abilities), and this enjoyment increases the more the capacity is realized, or the greater its complexity." We are motivated then (or, more exactly, it is a "natural fact that we have a tendency to be motivated") to develop our capacities and derive enjoyment from complex activities that fall within a more or less rational plan of life. Moreover, realizing our own good depends on being motivated in this fashion.

Considering Rawls's account of what goodness is, what rationality means, and the Aristotelian principle, we can now turn to Rawls's thin theory of the good. The primary goods that the contractors use to make their choices between candidate principles of justice are exactly the kinds of goods that persons require in order to realize their rational plans of life. These goods are "thin" in the sense that they alone do not determine what the good is for a person. As we discussed earlier, the good of a person is determined by what they choose for themselves with deliberative rationality. However, the primary goods, while not sufficient to determine the good for a person, are nevertheless necessary for a person to carry out any plan of life. In contrast, a "thick" notion of the good is precisely a claim about what constitutes the good for someone. Furthermore, since persons are motivated by the Aristotelian principle, they seek primary goods because it is these goods that they need to enhance and develop their capacities for achieving their own good. Thus, we can say that the primary goods are connected, in the most fundamental way, to the sort of creatures we are as human beings.

We should make one further point before moving on. The contractors do not derive the principles of justice from purely rational grounds. The introduction of the primary goods (and the accompanying account of the nature of persons) is essential to the argument for the principles. It is both rationality and the thin notion of the good that together yield the two principles.

THE PRIORITY OF THE RIGHT

Now that we have the above account of rationality and the good in place we can explain what Rawls means by stating that the right has priority over the good. Broadly, permissible conceptions of the good for citizens in a well-ordered society are those that fit with the two principles of justice. For such citizens their conception of the good is good *only if* it conforms to the principles of justice. A plan of life is an attempt to realize a conception of the good. Thus, plans of life are constrained and limited by the principles of right derived in the original position. Therefore, a conception of the good aimed at denying some citizens of their equal rights and liberties would be impermissible because it breached the first principle. This is so even if the good in question was something like happiness or well-being. For instance, we can imagine a politician arguing that greater general economic welfare was possible if citizens sacrificed some of their political freedom such as the freedom of association needed for support of employee unions. However, since the principles forbid sacrifices of this kind because of the lexical priority of the first principle, the principles of right trump the good of happiness.

The Problem of Stability

A stable society is one where citizens take themselves to have reason to abide by the principles of justice that govern its basic institutions. Egoists, for example, who view principles of justice as obstacles to their own advantage (unless cooperation happens to suit their schemes) will be tempted to free-ride on the cooperative efforts of others. Nonegoists who doubt the convictions of their fellow citizens may also conclude that abiding by principles of justice requires too much of a risk of sacrifice to be rational. A society where the general motivation to be just is lacking among citizens is unstable for Rawls. We saw earlier that the contractors think that it is not rational to enter into agreements that they believe the parties will defect from. So what we need is an argument for stability.

Rawls needs to show that having a sense of justice is part of a rational plan, of life for citizens in a democratic society. Such an argument will achieve its aim because if having a sense of justice is indeed part of a rational life plan, then being just is part of the objective good of citizens. If he can make this argument, then he has shown that the right and the good are in congruence in the right way. A sense of justice, as we spelled it out earlier, is the willingness to abide by principles of justice to which one has agreed (provided others are likewise willing). Citizens who have an effective sense of justice, in a society of others with an effective sense of justice, will not succumb to the temptation to free-ride on the cooperative efforts of their fellow citizens. Furthermore, their sense of justice will be reinforced as they recognize the mutual advantages that their joint cooperation renders to themselves and society as a whole. Rawls states (TJ: 436): "The most stable conception of justice, therefore, is presumably one that is perspicuous to our reason, congruent with our good, and rooted not in abnegation but in affirmation of the self." We have shown how for Rawls the principles of justice are made perspicuous to our reason through the device of the original position. Now we need to say more precisely how the principles are "congruent with our good." The hint for Rawls's answer is in the last sentence in the above quotation. As citizens of a democratic society, our self-conception is of ourselves as free and equal. Rawls interprets this as meaning that our foundational conception of ourselves is as autonomous agents in the Kantian sense of being free from the authority of history and our circumstances. We conceive ourselves as self-governing agents who give to ourselves the principles by which we live. Thus, we understand ourselves as able to rise above our particular circumstances and make choices as free agents. This self-conception as autonomous agents takes priority. Rawls argues (TJ: 503): "It is acting from this precedence that expresses our freedom from contingency and happenstance. Therefore in order to realize our nature we have no alternative but to plan to preserve our sense of justice as governing our other aims." Thus, our sense of justice has a privileged place in a rational plan of life. Indeed, it is the governing center of a rational life plan since it gives expression to our autonomy, the realization of which is the realization of our nature. The two principles of justice derived from the original position treasure and give priority to citizens' freedom and equality and are thus precisely the kinds of principles that autonomous agents would embrace as expressing their nature.

In conclusion, if a sense of justice is indeed part of a rational life plan, then the real and objective good of persons is achieved by acting in accord with the principles of justice. The right and the good are therefore congruent and thus we have reason to be obedient to the principles of justice. Since this argument holds for all citizens, it follows that a society governed by such principles is stable since everyone has reason to abide by the principles.

For reasons we will examine at length in part two, Rawls will be unhappy with this argument. In particular, he will be unhappy with the claims he makes about autonomy and the Kantian interpretation of autonomy he relies on to make the above argument.

5. Objections and Responses

A Theory of Justice is the subject of an enormous critical literature. It would require a separate book of some length to survey and assess the many criticisms and objections that have been made. It is a measure of the book's importance that so many philosophers have engaged with its ideas and continue to do so more than thirty years after its publication. In the sections that follow I touch on some of the criticisms that first-time readers of *A Theory of Justice* often make themselves, as well as some of the standard objections in the philosophical literature. I have organized the criticisms according to the broad perspectives from which they are made and I follow each set of criticisms with a response. My purpose in these sections is not to defend Rawls but rather to help readers engage more fully with his ideas through the back-and-forth of critical debate.

The Libertarian Argument

Libertarians take individual freedom very seriously. Their objections to *A Theory of Justice* rest on the claim that Rawls's theory does not fully respect the liberty of the individual. We will consider three interconnected objections. First, libertarians argue that desert is the central concept in a theory of justice and not fairness. Second, they argue that individuals have a right to self-ownership and to the benefits of self-ownership and that Rawls denies this. Third, they argue that Rawls's account of distributive justice undermines a properly robust account of private property. Therefore, according to the libertarian argument, Rawls's account of justice fails to give citizens what they deserve, denies their right to self-ownership, and contains an anemic notion of private property.

DESERT

We can begin with a modified version of a thought experiment from Robert Nozick (1974). Imagine a group of students who are asked to decide how to distribute grades on a scale of 0 to100. Suppose that there are ten students and 500 grade points to distribute. Let us assume further that 50 points are needed to pass the class (and they want to pass it) and that, although they have done the work for the course, none know how hard they have worked or how talented they are at the subject they are studying. Suppose further that the students are behind a veil of ignorance that prevents them from knowing their study habits and talents and that the grade points stand in for Rawls's primary goods. It is obvious that the students would choose to distribute the grade points equally since this would prevent any one of them failing the course and thus, suffering the worst outcome. An equal distribution would also ensure that each achieved the best worst outcome, namely, passing the course, although not doing very well. Of course, each would prefer to get a greater allocation of grade points than 50 (in fact each would prefer 100 points), but an equal distribution ensures that no student can be made better off (getting more than 50 points) without making someone else worse off (failing the course).

There is no question that the students would choose an equal distribution in an "original position" of this sort but the question is do they choose it because this is the correct way to choose or because of the peculiar circumstances of their situation? Nozick invites us to ask whether the students get what they *deserve* and the answer seems to be no. We would say that what they deserve depends on their work and the quality of this depends on their effort as well as their talents. These are facts particular to the individuals involved and are anchored in what they have done in the past and in their natural endowments. When students are prevented from knowing these facts they are forced into making choices that fail to reflect what they are entitled to. In other words, they are prevented from making a distribution of grade points that reflects what they *deserve*.

The analogy to the original position is obvious. The veil of ignorance prevents the contractors from knowing facts about themselves such as their natural talents and their levels of initiative and willingness to work hard. The criticism is that by making the contractors ignorant of these facts about themselves the original position nullifies an essential part of what justice means, namely, that citizens in a just society have only what they deserve. If the veil of ignorance prevents the contractors from determining what citizens deserve then the theory is incomplete at best or simply wrong at worst.

The criticism gains additional bite for some critics of Rawls when they reflect that the worst-off citizens in a Rawlsian society might receive a share of the primary goods that is greater in proportion than their "contribution to society." This is so because the best-off citizens may only enjoy their unequal share of society's wealth if the least well-off also benefit and this is true even if the least well-off do nothing to contribute to the greater wealth. Indeed, some readers of Rawls are offended by the idea that the best-off in society might have to forego some benefit that they "deserve" and give over this benefit to another "undeserving" person.

The appeal is to our intuition that justice must take into account what citizens deserve and insofar as Rawls's theory of justice, and, in particular, the original position, fail to capture this important intuition, Rawls's theory fails.

SELF-OWNERSHIP

Connected to the idea of desert is the claim that citizens own their natural assets. The idea of self-ownership has a long history in liberal thought. John Locke argued that it was through the use of our own labor power that unowned things became the private property of individual persons. He claimed that "mixing" one's labor with an unowned object and thereby improving it entitled one to exclusive use of it and the benefits of that use. Aside from the dubious metaphysics of Locke's argument, it does appeal to a strong intuition that we have a special claim to our natural assets—our intelligence, talents, and aptitudes. After all, if *we* do not own them, who does?

As we have seen, Rawls prevents the contractors from knowing what their natural assets are. By doing so, he prevents them from choosing principles of justice that favor citizens with particular talents and disfavoring citizens with other assets. The result of this is that the benefits that accrue from the exercise of citizens' natural talents are pooled and distributed in accordance with the difference principle. Rawls's argument for placing natural assets behind the veil of ignorance is the same as the argument for all the other items of knowledge he conceals from the contractors. He regards natural assets as undeserved and thus arbitrary from the moral point of view. Like our starting place in society our native intelligence, talents, and aptitudes are the result of the "lottery of birth." Thus, why should we benefit from mere luck and why should those who are unlucky be deprived?

There are a great many difficult philosophical questions that surround this debate. For example, if my intelligence, talents, and aptitudes are subtracted from me what, if anything, is left of me? Have we not subtracted my identity as a person and how can who I am be arbitrary from a moral point of view? At this point, however, I want to focus on the criticism that citizens are entitled to the benefits that flow from the use of their natural assets because they own themselves and therefore they have a basic right to the use of their natural assets and to benefit from them. The problem for Rawls is that the difference principle strips citizens of this right and forces them to use their talents, if they use them at all, for the benefit of others. If self-ownership is a fundamental moral fact about us and, if Rawls fails to acknowledge this fact in the original position, then there is something seriously wrong with the principles that emerge from it. In particular, something is amiss with the difference principle that distributes the benefits of social cooperation. In short, Rawls socializes citizens' capacities and denies that these capacities are private, whereas the claim against him is that citizens' capacities are morally protected and private.

PRIVATE PROPERTY

The final criticism from the libertarian perspective claims that Rawls's account of justice has a weak notion of private property. We should be clear that Rawls argues that citizens have a basic right to personal property and distinguishes this from private ownership of what Marx called the "means of production." The latter kind of property is used to produce goods and services and from which profit is made (if the enterprise is successful). Rawls is clear in *A Theory of Justice* that the exact type of just economic system is not determined behind the veil of ignorance in the original position (although some are ruled out). While it is apparent enough that a Rawlsian society will be a property-owning democracy or a form of democratic socialism, the exact claims and entitlements citizens have to ownership of the means of production and to the benefits of such ownership is settled in the constitutional phase of negotiations. For some critics this gives insufficient normative weight to property rights. Roughly following Nozick's argument here, we can summarize the criticisms by saying that justice demands that citizens are entitled to the use and benefit of a piece of property (including ownership of the means of production) if a citizen acquired that property justly in the first place, or had it transferred to her by someone else who had acquired it justly.

Broadly speaking, a person acquires an item of property justly if she acquires it without coercion or fraud. This entitlement theory of justice denies that private property is something that can be *distributed* as if it were "manna from heaven," as Nozick says. All justly held property is owned by someone who is entitled to it, and if it, or the benefits of owning it, are taken away from him then he suffers an injustice. Any distribution is just provided it comes about through just acquisitions and transactions. The alleged mistake that Rawls makes is to treat private property as distributable and thus, to ignore citizens' entitlements.

One cause of this alleged error is that the original position prevents the contractors considering the history of the distribution of the ownership of resources since the veil of ignorance prevents the contractors knowing the historical particulars of their society. What the contractors do consider is how different principles of distributive justice allocate bundles of primary goods and they make a choice between these allocations given the very limited knowledge they have and their interest in maximizing their share of these goods. The principle they choose, the difference principle, reflects the fact that they apply the maximin rule and seek the best worst outcome and therefore privilege the perspective of the least-advantaged. The best-off are permitted an unequal share of primary goods only if the worst-off benefit too. However, this arrangement presupposes that the best-off have only a weak claim to their private property. The criticism gains extra traction when it is pointed out that Rawls's approach to this question already excludes from consideration a theory of justice like the entitlement theory.

In summary, the criticism is that Rawls has a normatively weak account of private property. Unlike the entitlement theory which maximally protects citizens' rights in all private property Rawls allows that nonpersonal private property in a just society can be redistributed to meet the requirements of the difference principle.

RESPONSE TO THE LIBERTARIAN ARGUMENT

Rawls himself does not engage directly with the particulars of these objections. Thus we will have to extract Rawlsian responses from his texts rather than simply rehearse Rawls's own arguments. This is the case for the most of the responses to criticisms from other perspectives as well. The criticisms from the libertarian perspective are closely connected and I will deal with them together.

The intuitive appeal of the idea of desert as a foundational concept for a theory of justice is no more than an intuitive appeal. As we recall, Rawls's account of justification in *A Theory of Justice*, reflective equilibrium, requires us to subject our initial intuitions about justice to scrutiny and to make adjustments. Now, it would be odd if justice as fairness had no place at all for the notion of desert and so we need to locate its place in Rawls's thinking and distinguish it from the notion of desert at work in the criticism we are examining. Rawls thinks of desert as "legitimate expectation" (TJ: 89) and the question for him is what makes citizens' expectations legitimate? The answer to this question is that the two principles, in arranging the background conditions that inform the workings of a society's basic institutions, define for citizens which of their expectations are legitimate. For example, the best-off in a Rawlsian society have a legitimate expectation of a greater share of primary goods when the requirements of the difference principle have been met. The worst-off are better off than they would be under an equal distribution of primary goods. The best-off have a legitimate expectation and thus for Rawls's they *deserve* their unequal share. In the same way, all citizens deserve an equal respect for their political rights protected under the greatest equal liberty principle. Therefore, Rawls clearly has a notion of desert and so it is false that citizens in a Rawlsian society do not get what they deserve.

This, though, is only part of a response to the criticism. The larger claim is that the notion of desert only makes sense when it is embedded in some account of legitimacy. The criticism of Rawls we canvassed above has a different account of legitimacy but this is not a telling criticism of Rawls in the absence of a defense of this different account. The grade-point thought experiment gains its purchase on our assent because of its appeal to an unexamined and implicit account of the legitimacy of expectations. Rawls's theory of justice is radical in the sense that it aims to build an account of political and distributive justice from the ground up. It begins with our intuitions and our inherited, historical ideas and ideals and through a process of self-examination, critical reflection, and re-articulation constructs a refashioned assembly of concepts and principles. Once we make what is implicit explicit (as the method of reflective equilibrium demands of us) then we might favor the alternative Rawlsian account of desert. There is not a primitive ideal of desert to which all theories of justice are beholden and the grade-point thought experiment does presuppose such a primitive ideal.

The second criticism that claims Rawls fails to acknowledge the principle of self-ownership is subject to a similar set of replies. First, we should be wary of the very idea of owning oneself. If this is meant as a simple fact about us it seems to be false. The idea of ownership belongs within a network of institutions that define laws and rules of property ownership. In the absence of these political and social institutions the very notion of ownership makes no sense. A Rawlsian will resist the claim that there is a primitive ideal of self-ownership and that a theory of justice has to be committed to persons *owning* themselves. However, there is a strong intuitive appeal to the idea that we have a special claim or relationship to our natural assets and we would expect a theory of justice to be responsive to this appeal.

For Rawls a part of the response to the criticism lies in the first of the two principles where he sets out the basic rights and freedoms citizens are entitled to. One of these rights is a right to the integrity of the person which includes, of course, bodily integrity. This right protects citizens from being used by others without their informed consent. Our intelligence, talents, and aptitudes are therefore protected in the strongest possible way in Rawls's theory. The second step of the criticism, though, is one that Rawls resists. It is argued that citizens are entitled to all the benefits of the use of their natural talents. This, however, does not follow from the fact that we have a right to the integrity of the person. The extent of our entitlement to these benefits depends on what principles organize and inform the workings of the basic institutions of society. It is these background conditions that define what benefits citizens have entitlement to, including the benefits that flow from the use of their natural assets. Once we separate out the right to the integrity of the person from questions concerning the distribution of the benefits of the use of natural talents, then the forcefulness of the criticism diminishes. Redistributing such benefits does not necessarily mean that citizens' bodies are being used as a mere means for the benefit of others. Thus, Rawls distinguishes between the right to personal and bodily integrity and the question of how the benefits of social cooperation are to be distributed.

Therefore, when Rawls argues that our natural talents are undeserved and are arbitrary from the moral point of view, he means only that we have no a priori legitimate expectation to be the exclusive beneficiaries of their exercise. This is not to say that our personal identity is morally arbitrary and nor is it to say that we should never be the beneficiaries of the use of our natural talents. Indeed, Rawls allows that talented and industrious persons should have the incentive of a greater share of society's wealth, provided that all benefit to some degree (as required by the difference principle).

Finally, with respect to self-ownership, we should mention that natural assets are only assets in circumstances favorable to the particular forms of intelligence, talents, and aptitudes a person has. Natural assets are embedded in political, social, and material circumstances and are rewarded or penalized by a particular arrangement of social institutions. A talent for baseball or a knack for philosophy is "natural" only in a limited sense. Having terrific hand-eye coordination might not be an asset among a community of philosophers and an aptitude for philosophical debate will not hit many home runs.

Now we can turn to the place of private property in Rawls's theory. It is true that the entitlement theory of just acquisition we canvassed earlier strongly denies what Rawls asserts. Namely, justice demands that property be distributed according to a pattern and that no one be entitled to own property unless it is in accord with the pattern of distribution defined by the difference principle. A citizen's claim to ownership of private property is therefore weaker than the claim someone would have under an entitlement theory where an absolute right to ownership follows from showing that a piece of property was "acquired justly" or "transferred to her justly." Rawls's response requires us to look at his theory as a whole and not merely focus on the difference principle. The greatest equal liberty principle is lexically prior to the difference principle. This fact is crucial to understanding Rawls's account of private property. Citizens' status as political equals and as having a fundamental claim to equal freedom are both prior ideals to the question of how private property is distributed. In other words, the question of property distribution is subordinate to the question of how rights to equality and freedom are secured. It follows that any account of legitimate property ownership that did not support and foster the prior ideals of democratic citizenship would be rejected.

Two somewhat lengthy arguments would need to be made at this point to establish, first, that the difference principle did indeed support the ideals of democratic citizenship and, second, that an entitlement theory did not. At this stage though, we will have to content ourselves with the following short argument. Suppose there was a moment where everyone held their property justly in accordance with the entitlement theory and suppose further that we accept any distribution that followed provided citizens freely transferred their property, thus preserving the "justice" of everyone's holdings. The problem, according to Rawls, is that over time considerable disparities in wealth may occur and these disparities will undermine the values enshrined in the lexically prior first principle. Rawls argues that (JF: 53):

> Even though the initial state may have been just, and subsequent social conditions may also have been just for some time, the accumulated results of many separate and seemingly fair agreements entered into by individuals and associations are likely over an extended period to undermine the background conditions required for free and fair agreements. Very considerable wealth and property may accumulate in a few hands, and these concentrations are likely to undermine fair equality of opportunity, the fair value of political liberties, and so on.

Thus, the contractors in the original position treasure their freedom and equality and give priority to the realization of these values. They regard primary goods only as means for the exercise of their freedoms and for securing their political equality. The question of what is to count as legitimate private property thus arises in a context of how to create the background conditions for preserving the full value of democratic citizenship over time.

We can conclude by stating that Rawls views the question of private property ownership and the problem of distributive justice as a subordinate part of the broader issue of justice. He regards the rights and liberties of democratic citizenship as having a stronger normative claim than claims of property ownership. An opponent will not be satisfied with this response if he disagrees with Rawls on the place of democratic citizenship. However, my main purpose here has been to show that it is a mistake to focus just on the difference principle and that Rawls's account of distributive justice gains in plausibility when we take, as we should, the wider view of his theory.

Finally, one further Rawlsian reason for being wary of a theory of justice that allows for great disparities in wealth is that when society is viewed as system of cooperation for mutual advantage then such disparities undermine both the idea of cooperation and the notion of mutual advantage. For those who are best-off in a Rawlsian society they at least have the advantage of knowing that their fellow citizens recognize and acknowledge their entitlement to their benefits. It seems unlikely, as a matter of empirical fact, that a society in which there is great disparity of wealth, which impacts on citizens' freedoms and equality, will be regarded as a place of cooperation and mutual advantage by the least advantaged. If nothing else, the best-off under a Rawlsian scheme of property ownership will be secure in their advantages since the worst-off will acknowledge their right to their privileges.

The Feminist Argument

Susan Okin (1987) argues that Rawls's account of justice fails to incorporate the causes and consequences of gender and sex discrimination. The argument is directed at two levels. First, Okin says that Rawls's method and theoretical construction ignores gender as a significant part of a theory of justice and, furthermore, presupposes in its language and assumptions a traditional gender division in society. Second, once we do take gender into account we will see that social institutions, the family in particular, would require significant intervention to make them comply with the two principles.

Okin's first complaint is Rawls's extensive use of gendered language that exclusively favors the male pronoun and talk of fathers and sons rather than mothers and daughters. Moreover, Rawls speaks of the contractors as "heads of households" and goes on refer to these as "he" and so entrenches in the reader's mind a traditional understanding of the family and a woman's subordinate place in it. Okin writes (45): "Thus there is a certain blindness to the sexism of the tradition in which Rawls is a participant, which tends to render his terms of reference even more ambiguous than they might otherwise be. A feminist reader finds it difficult not to keep asking: 'Does this theory of justice apply to women or not?'"

The "blindness" she describes extends beyond the surface language of *A Theory of Justice* into the method itself. In Rawls's list of what lies behind the veil of ignorance gender is not explicitly one of the items. If injustices and inequality in society track a citizen's gender then we would expect gender to lie behind the veil of ignorance since we would not want principles tailored to gender interests any more than we would want them tailored to class interests. From a feminist perspective we might think that either Rawls does not recognize these sources of injustice or that he does not think them important.

A third source of criticism is Rawls's presuppositions concerning the family. The family is one of the basic institutions in society. It is important as far as justice is concerned for a number of reasons including the psychological development of morally competent citizens. More generally, how children fare in families has a profound affect on citizens' life prospects in the wider society. However, Okin argues, Rawls does not apply the principles of justice to relations between family members, thereby allowing that, in its internal relations, one of the basic institutions of society might be unjust. Furthermore, Rawls assumes that citizens enter into wage labor markets but family labor, including the rearing and moral education of children is unpaid labor and, she says, often not recognized as labor at all. Since women most often do this kind of family work they fall from the view of Rawls's account of justice. There is also no recognition of the power relations within families that often lead to the dependence of women on men precisely because they do their work within the family. In general, Rawls fails to consider the sexual division of labor.

RESPONSE TO THE FEMINIST ARGUMENT

A Theory of Justice, published in 1971, does employ gendered language that with contemporary eyes looks like a notable fault of composition in a book on social justice. However, a sympathetic reader will remember the date and period of its publication and ask whether the theory itself entails a gender bias when we look beyond the language of the text. Rawls writes in a footnote in the 1997 essay "The Idea of Public Reason Revisited" (reprinted in *The Law of Peoples*: 156) that: "I have thought that J.S. Mill's *The Subjection of Women* . . . made clear that a decent liberal conception of justice (including what I call justice as fairness) implied equal justice for women as well as men. Admittedly, *A Theory of Justice* should have been more explicit about this." Moving on to the second criticism, Rawls clearly agrees with Okin that in the list of items of knowledge to be placed behind the veil of ignorance knowledge of the contractor's gender ought to have been included. Rawls includes sex as one of the "contingencies" not relevant from the moral point of view in a 1975 article and so corrects the error. More explicitly, Rawls includes "sex" as one of the items behind the veil of ignorance in *Justice as Fairness*, his final book, published in 2001. This amendment or clarification of the theory clearly addresses the question of whether Rawls thought questions of gender belonged among the considerations of the contractors in the original position.

The more serious feminist challenge addresses the role of the family in *A Theory of Justice.* Rawls does use the phrase "head of household" with its implications of a particular structure and form of family life. He understands the family in a functionalist way. What matters is that the family, as an institution, support and sustain the requirements of democratic citizenship, in particular the development of a sense of justice in children. Therefore, as Rawls makes explicit in later writings, where he says that (JF: 163): "no particular form of the family (monogamous, heterosexual, or otherwise) is so far required by a political conception of justice so long as it is arranged to fulfill these tasks effectively and does not run afoul of other political values." The contractors need to *represent* a family in order to give them a perspective on society as an ongoing, intergenerational, concern and thus to give them a view of their interests that extends beyond themselves but remains *their* interests.

Rawls disagrees with Okin on her claim that the two principles ought to be applied to the family and thus to relations between members of the family. Families are often the site of unequal power relations, and unpaid and unrecognized labor. While it is true that these inequalities are almost always marked by gender it is not clear how justice principles could be applied to familial relations and whether this would be desirable. Rawls has two responses to Okin's argument. His first is that the justice principles do not, and should not, apply to the internal workings of every social institution. They do not, for example, apply to universities or churches that have hierarchical rather than democratic internal structures. However, the two principles function as constraints on the effects of the internal workings of the family. Therefore, what matters for Rawls, once again, is citizens' capacities for democratic citizenship. If relations between family members are detrimental to a citizen's ability to function as an equal member of the political community or to pursue a rational plan of life then these are grounds for intervention in the life of the family. Spousal abuse and child neglect are obvious examples where the perspective of justice supersedes the narrower perspective of family life. Rawls's second point is merely to say that "at some point society has to trust to the natural affection and goodwill of parents" (JF: 165). Many feminists will balk at this claim since, they argue, it is precisely affection and goodwill that provide the grounds for the exploitation of women within families. However, the issue turns on whether Rawls's claim that the external constraints of justice are sufficient will satisfy feminist concerns about the family.

The Communitarian Argument

The criticisms from the communitarian perspective focus on Rawls's account of identity and agency and on his account of community. Rawls's full response to the latter criticisms can only be made once we have examined his arguments in *Political Liberalism* in part two where he develops the theory of an "overlapping consensus" that explains how a political community can exist where citizens subscribe to different conceptions of the good. We will return therefore to the communitarian critique of Rawls when we look at the criticisms of *Political Liberalism.* At this stage, we will focus on communitarian criticisms of Rawls's conception of the self and say something in a preliminary way about the problem of community for Rawls.

THE ABSTRACTED SELF—IDENTITY AND AGENCY

Michael Sandel (1982) argues that Rawls's conception of the self in *A Theory of Justice* is "metaphysically embarrassing" (Sandel: 14). It is argued by Sandel and other communitarians that the account of justice and the self that Rawls develops is based on notions of identity and agency that are flawed. Sandel alleges that Rawls conceives of the self as separable from her social and historical identity, her ends and purposes, and her relations with others. It this self, unencumbered by any particular identity, not situated in either family or community and without a role in society that "chooses" principles of justice in the original position. Communitarians question whether it makes any sense at all to think of the self in this way. For them, a person's identity just is the accumulated particulars of her past and circumstances together with her aims and ends. There is no self that is independent of her community because it is the community that *makes* the self. Thus, for Sandel, Rawls's notion of the self is "incoherent."

Therefore, Rawls's contractors in the original position cannot make genuine choices and cannot display genuine agency. The only basis for making choices that they could have is the unexamined desire for "more rather than less"; what Sandel calls the "self as subject of possession" (Sandel: 54), one whose creed is "mine not yours, mine not me" (Sandel: 55). This desire to possess is left unexamined because the means to step back and reflect on whether this or that desire is worthy or good is denied to the contractors because it is precisely the particulars of a person's life and her circumstances that enable her to scrutinize and evaluate her desires. Instead of the ideal of the self as someone who makes "choices" in this way, Sandel and other communitarians advance an ideal of self-discovery.

Thus, the very notion of what justice requires becomes distorted, it is argued, when it is thought of as a matter of distributing bundles of goods between "atomistic," self-regarding, citizens. M.W. Jackson (1985) has argued that how goods in society ought to be distributed depends crucially on who particular people are. From the Aristotelian point of view he advocates, Jackson says that the question of distribution is not merely a matter of dividing quantities of primary goods between citizens. What matters instead is that citizens strive towards developing their particular capacities and aim at the excellence that they are best fitted for. This means that how goods are distributed requires detailed knowledge of who citizens are and what their situations entail. Therefore, the proper subject of justice is not only the institutions comprising the basic structure but individuals and their lives and characters as well. If we abstract from these individuals when we consider the fundamental principles of justice, then we miss the major part of what justice demands.

In summary, there are two main complaints against Rawls. First, the abstracted self is a philosophical fiction and such a self cannot make meaningful choices between candidate principles of justice precisely because this self is denied the means for making such a choice. Second, that the problem of distribution, as Rawls understands it, is secondary to the more fundamental question of allocating goods to enable citizens to live their lives well in accordance with their capacities and potential for excellence.

COMMUNITY

The communitarian response to *A Theory of Justice* focuses on the place of community in Rawls's theory. There are two main criticisms. First, it is argued that Rawls has no account of a common good that would support a properly robust notion of community. Second, it is argued that the Kantian account of the good that he does offer is inadequate for, indeed, undermining of, the idea of community.

It will be useful to begin with the account of community that Rawls does give before looking at these complaints in more detail. Unlike some other contractarians and liberals Rawls is alert to the need for a substantive account of community in a theory of justice. He contrasts what he calls the idea "private society" with the notion of community. The former conceives of society as an arena purely for the pursuit of individual, private, and usually competing ends. Society's institutions are regarded only as facilitators of these pursuits and not as having any value on their own account. Finally, society as a whole likewise has no value apart from the extent to which it efficiently allows individuals to realize their goals. Rawls strongly rejects the idea of a "private society" and emphasizes what he calls the "social nature of mankind." What then are the forms of sociability and community in a just society according to Rawls? He first identifies social unions as the basic form of community. These unions have "shared final ends and common activities valued for themselves" (TJ: 460). Churches and universities are good examples of social unions (as well as families and friendships). The congregation of a church shares the aims and purposes of its religion and value its collective activities of prayer and charity work, and so on. There is a common sense of the good attached to a social union (and when this common sense breaks down so too does the union).

The next step for Rawls is to argue that a well-ordered society is a "social union of social unions." In other words, a just society is a community of communities. What does this mean? What are the shared ends and valued collective activities that constitute the common good of citizens in a well-ordered society? We have to tread carefully because there is a disanalogy between Rawls's account of a social union and his account of the social union of social unions. The former have a thick conception of the good (a shared set of religious beliefs and practices, for example) whereas the latter has only a thin conception of the good. What Rawls has in mind is that the "collective activity of justice is the preeminent form of human flourishing" (TJ: 463). In other words, citizens collectively value as their common good the principles of justice they subscribe to and the institutions that instantiate them. What they effectively value then is, as we saw earlier, themselves and their fellow citizens as free and equal and the institutions that define and promote these values. Therefore, citizens in a just democratic society value the idea of themselves and others following rational plans of life as autonomous agents without saying that any *particular* rational plan of life is the good for *all* citizens. Citizens in a democratic society have different conceptions of the good although they are all committed to the good of what is right and just. This is a real and important distinction although Rawls at this point has not yet developed the vocabulary to make it clear, which he does in *Political Liberalism*.

This is Rawls's account of community in *A Theory of Justice*. With the idea of a union of social unions he attempts to mark out a path *between* the idea of society as private and the idea of a community as requiring everyone to subscribe to the same substantive conception of the good. Rawls will keep the main elements of this account of community in place. In later writings he will reinterpret and revise parts of it. However, we can rehearse, briefly, some of the communitarian arguments against Rawls's account of community.

The first argument claims that a political community requires a substantive shared conception of the good and that Rawls's idea of a social union of social unions is not a thick enough conception of the good to anchor a community. Different communitarian thinkers will advocate different ideas about what the shared good of a society should be and how thick it should be. Democratic communitarians such as Richard Rorty argue that it is democratic values which emerge in particular histories of Western societies that count as the shared substantive good. However, in general, communitarians are critical of Rawls's account of community in *A Theory of Justice* because, they argue, a genuine community shares a set of substantial values that emerge from the shared history and circumstances of its members. A joint commitment of citizens to the two principles and to institutions that instantiate them is, in their opinion, not sufficient to anchor a genuine community.

The criticism above is part of a general critique of liberalism that promotes the primacy and value of community over that of the individual, as we saw earlier in the communitarian critique of Rawls's notions of self and agency. The second argument is more particular in focusing on what Rawls in *A Theory of Justice* does take to be a shared value, namely the value of individual autonomy and choice. For reasons we have already examined, communitarians regard this value to be a distortion of a true human flourishing because it promotes the ideal of citizens as possessive individuals floating freely above their social and historical circumstances. Thus, even if we were to grant that Rawls does have shared value that he takes to be substantive enough, namely the value of autonomy, he is mistaken because this value cannot do the work of uniting individuals into a community. Furthermore, for some communitarians, the ideal of autonomy is not only a philosophical error but it is also a practical evil. They complain that actual communities are fragmented and threatened by liberal ideals of individual autonomy. Overall, based on the communitarian argument, either Rawls's account of community lacks the required shared common set of values and purposes or what Rawls takes to be a common value is inadequate to task of anchoring a genuine sense of community.

RESPONSE TO THE COMMUNITARIAN IDEA

The claim that Rawls has a deficient conception of the self and agency rests on what I think is a misunderstanding and misreading of *A Theory of Justice*. Rawls does have a substantive and historically located conception of self. He does, after all, specify that he is constructing a theory of justice for a particular kind of historically specific society; namely, a modern liberal democratic society. He regards his method for arriving at the two principles as a process of "self-understanding" undertaken by citizens of such a society. The mistake that the communitarian critique makes is to confuse citizens with the contractors in the original position. Rawls clearly does not think of the contractors either as metaphysical descriptions of the self or as models or ideals of the self. We, as citizens of democratic societies and the audience for Rawls's account of justice, are not "really" abstracted and historically unanchored contractors. The original position is a device for modeling a choice situation that perspicuously exhibits the main features of our moral and political framework. There are no metaphysical commitments here to what we are "really." Thus, the contractors are abstractions from citizens but do not represent an "incoherent" theory of the self. Any theory of justice must abstract to some degree from "flesh and blood" individuals in marking out what is important and relevant to consider when thinking about what justice requires. A virtue of Rawls's method is that he makes very clear just what is abstracted through his description of the original position. Part of the problem is that we are encouraged to think of the self as either totally embedded in its circumstances or as an abstraction unconnected to reality. If we reject the latter then we find ourselves committed to the former. Rawls rejects this false dualism and his theory is, in part, an argument for a conception of the self that is anchored in its circumstances but not a hostage to them. We have a capacity for autonomy and for constructing and realizing a rational plan of life. We also find ourselves in particular circumstances that form the environment in which choices are made and possibilities recognized. Rawls's theory captures this double aspect of democratic citizens' lives; their freedom and their "situatedness."

The argument that Rawls's theory has an inadequate account of community will be addressed more fully in part two. I do want to point out that the communitarian criticism of Rawls supposes that a political community is a social union with a shared set of substantive values and purposes. The alternative to this idea of community can only be what Rawls calls a private society that has no shared values. Thus either a political community, properly understood, is modeled on a family or church or it is a mere collection of atomistic individuals who gather for their own convenience. Rawls once again rejects the dualism this criticism implies. However, his argument in *A Theory of Justice* is undeveloped in many important ways. We can only fully appreciate Rawls's ideas of community and the place and role of shared values once we have examined the idea of a *political* liberalism.

For Further Reading on *A Theory of Justice*

Barry, B. 1973. *The Liberal Theory of Justice: A Critical Examination of the Principal Doctrines in* A Theory of Justice *by John Rawls.* Oxford: Clarendon Press.

Barry, B. 1973. John Rawls and the Priority of Liberty. *Philosophy and Public Affairs* 2: 274–90.

Beauchamp, T. 1980. Distributive Justice and the Difference Principal. In *John Rawls's Theory of Social Justice,* ed. H. Gene Blocker and Elizabeth H. Smith, 132–61. Athens: Ohio University Press.

Buchanan, A. 1989. Assessing the Communitarian Critique of Liberalism. *Canadian Journal of Philosophy* 23: 75–99.

Clark, B., and Gintis, H. 1978. Rawlsian Justice and Economic Systems. *Philosophy and Public Affairs* 7 (4): 302–25.

Crocker, L. 1977. Equality, Solidarity and Rawls's Maximin. *Philosophy and Public Affairs* 6: 262–66.

Daniels, N. 1975. Equal Liberty and Unequal Worth of Liberty. In *Reading Rawls: Critical Studies on Rawls' A Theory of Justice*, ed. N. Daniels, 253–81. New York: Basic Books.

———. 1979. Wide Reflective Equilibrium and Theory Acceptance in Ethics. *Journal of Philosophy* 76: 256–82.

———, ed. 1989. *Reading Rawls.* New York: Basic Books.

Darwall, S. L. 1976. A Defense of the Kantian Interpretation. *Ethics* 86 (2): 164–70.

Dworkin, R. 1973. The Original Position. *University of Chicago Law Review* 40: 500–533.

English, J. 1977. Justice between Generations. *Philosophical Studies* 31: 91–104.

Gauthier, D. 1974. Justice and Natural Endowment: Toward a Critique of Rawls's Ideological Framework. *Social Theory and Practice* 3: 3–26.

Goldman, A. H. 1976. Rawls's Original Position and the Difference Principal. *Journal of Philosophy* 73: 845–49.

Hare, R. M. 1973. Rawls' Theory of Justice. *Philosophical Quarterly* 23: 144–55.

Hart, H. L. A. 1973. Rawls on Justice. *Ethics* 83: 294–307.

Harsanyi, J. 1975. Can the Maximin Principal Serve as a Basis for Morality? A Critique of John Rawls's Theory. *American Political Science Review* 69: 594–606.

Held, V. 1976. On Rawls and Self-Interest. *Midwest Studies in Philosophy* 1: 57–60.

Hill, T. E., Jr. 1989. Kantian Constructivism in Ethics. *Ethics* 99: 752–70.

———. 1994. The Problem of Stability in *Political Liberalism. Pacific Philosophy Quarterly* 75: 332–52.

Jackson, M. W. 1985. Aristotle on Rawls: A Critique of Quantitative Justice. *Journal of Value Inquiry* 19: 99–110.

Kukathas, C., and Philip, P. 1990. *Rawls: A Theory of Justice and Its Critics*, Stanford: Stanford University Press.

Laden, A. S. 2004. Taking the Distinction between Persons Seriously. *Journal of Moral Philosophy: An International Journal of Moral, Political and Legal Philosophy* 1: 277–92.

Lyons, D. 1972. Rawls versus Utilitarianism. *Journal of Philosophy* 69: 535–45.

Mandle, J. 1999. The Reasonable in Justice as Fairness. *Canadian Journal of Philosophy* 29: 75–107.

Miller, R. 1974. Rawls and Marxism. *Philosophy and Public Affairs* 3: 167–91.

Nagel, T. 1973. Rawls on Justice. *Philosophical Review* 82: 220–34.

Narveson, J. 1982. Rawls and Utilitarianism. In *The Limits of Utilitarianism*, ed. Harlan B. Miller and William H. Williams, 128–42. Minneapolis: University of Minnesota Press.

Nielsen, K. 1977. The Choice between Perfectionism and Rawlsian Contractarianism. *Interpretation* 6: 132–39.

Nozick, R. 1974. Distributive Justice. In his *Anarchy, State and Utopia*. New York: Basic Books, 149–231.

Okin, S. M. 1987. Justice and Gender. *Philosophy and Public Affairs* 16 (1): 42–72.

Pogge, T. 1981. The Kantian Interpretation of Justice as Fairness. *Zeitschrift für philosophische Forschung* 35: 47–65.

———. 1989. *Realizing Rawls*. Ithaca: Cornel University Press.

———. 1994. *John Rawls*. Munich: C.H. Beck.

———. 2007. *John Rawls: His Life and Theory of Justice*. Oxford: Oxford University Press.

Richardson, H., and Weithman, P. 1999. *The Philosophy of Rawls: A Collection of Essays*. 5 vols. New York: Garland.

Sandel, M. J. 1984. The Procedural Republic and the Unencumbered Self. *Political Theory* 12 (1): 81–96.

———. 1998. *Liberalism and the Limits of Justice*. Cambridge: Cambridge University Press.

Sen, A. 2006. What Do We Want from a Theory of Justice? *Journal of Philosophy* 103: 215–38.

Sterba, J. 1974. Justice as Desert. *Social Theory and Practice* 3: 101–16.

Talisse, R. B. 2001. *On Rawls: A Liberal Theory of Justice and Justification*. Belmont, CA: Wadsworth.

Taylor, R. S. 2003. Rawls's Defense of the Priority of Liberty: A Kantian Reconstruction. *Philosophy and Public Affairs* 31: 246–71.

Wolff, R. P. 1977. *Understanding Rawls*. Princeton, NJ: Princeton University Press.

Part Two
Political Liberalism

1. The Good in Political Liberalism

We ended part one with Rawls's account of the theoretical basis of the argument for the two principles. The final section of that account on the relation between the right and the good offered an argument for why citizens would regard having a sense of justice as part of a fully rational plan of life and why abiding by principles of justice is part of their "real good." This argument answered the difficult question of why citizens should be motivated to be just and it thereby addressed and solved the problem of stability. This latter problem concerns the stability of just basic institutions in a democratic society and required for its solution an adequate account of motivation for justice among citizens.

There is, however, a deep problem for Rawls's argument, and the theory of political liberalism is an attempt to address this problem. Citizens are regarded as having a higher-order interest in advancing and protecting their self-conception as free and equal persons, that is, as autonomous agents. The two principles achieve this end by giving priority to liberties and rights and by securing the means for citizens to act as autonomous agents. In fact, it is precisely this fit between the principles and this fundamental and foundational aspect of their self-understanding as autonomous persons that accounts for citizens' motivation to be just. Autonomy is a basic idea that secures the principles.

This raises some difficult issues. Autonomy is a good in the sense that it defines an ideal of personhood; it is both a metaphysical and a moral conception of the good of individuals. In Rawls's discussion of autonomy in *A Theory of Justice* he renders the idea of autonomy in its Kantian form. A critical reader would question Rawls at this point in the argument. Up to this moment we have been lead to believe that the theory eschews substantive conceptions of the good and relies on only a thin theory of the good. However, the good of Kantian autonomy looks very thick as far as goods go. It would seem then that the derivation of the principles of justice in the original position disguised a substantive, thick conception of the good after all. This is a problem for two reasons. First, the argument for the principles has to suppose that when the veil of ignorance is lifted citizens will all embrace the good of autonomy (in fact, not just autonomy but the Kantian interpretation of it). Therefore, acceptable conceptions of the good are in fact restricted in advance by an overarching Kantian liberal conception of the good. Second, if this supposition is not made, then Rawls's argument for the two principles is fatally inadequate on his own account of what counts as an adequate theory. Without the supposition of the general acceptance of liberal autonomy, Rawls has no argument for why citizens should be just, that is, abide by the principles they would agree to in the original position. Therefore, either the theory does presuppose a thick conception of the good (although Rawls says it does not in *A Theory of Justice*), or the justification of the principles is inadequate.

Rawls has a couple of options to resolve this issue (other than abandoning the theory altogether). He can argue for the good of liberal autonomy as an overarching conception of the good on either universalist or communitarian grounds, or he can provide a different theory of justification so as to account for the motivation among citizens to be just that does not presuppose the good of liberal autonomy. Rawls opts for the latter approach, as he must. To argue that the good of autonomy is a universal, transcendent good would undermine his nonfoundationalist, coherentist account of justification. If autonomy had such a transcendent status, then the aim of achieving reflective equilibrium would be to track and identify "the good," and we would need a separate argument to say why our merely agreeing to something tracked a metaphysically transcendent object. In other words, there are many reasons to avoid the metaphysically dubious claims of moral realism, not least of which is a concern with ontological parsimony and epistemic clarity. There are further conceptual and practical considerations for rejecting liberal universalism which we will examine in some detail below when we look at what Rawls calls the "problem of pluralism."

The liberal communitarian option is no more attractive for Rawls. The communitarian view argues that what makes a collection of individuals a community is a shared conception of the good. Insofar as democratic societies are communities at all it follows, for a communitarian, that they require a shared notion of the good. Moreover, communitarians generally argue that this shared notion lies embedded in the culture of communities. The role of the philosopher is to unearth and give expression to the norms and values that constitute the normative basis of a community. Thus, it could be argued that liberal autonomy stands as the normative basis of particular democratic societies and that the argument from the original position is an articulation and clarification of an actual shared conception of the good. There are a number of reasons Rawls wants to reject this approach. One reason is that he is suspicious of the idea that our values can be reduced to a *mere* historical inheritance and that although we can articulate these values more or less clearly we cannot transcend them (we cannot be self-authenticating sources of value). However, a more pressing criticism of the communitarian approach is the argument that communities have a single or common good and that this is what defines them as communities. Again, when we discuss pluralism in the next section we will see that Rawls rejects the claim of a common good as basis for the legitimate exercise for state power in democratic societies. He will offer an alternative definition of democratic community. Therefore, Rawls resists the argument that liberal autonomy can stand as the basis for the common good of democratic societies.

Political Conception of the Good

THE FACT OF PLURALISM

Rawls is not therefore going to defend a liberal conception of the good with autonomy as its centerpiece. He is going to accept a plurality of conceptions of the good (with some important limitations as we will see) and attempt a defense of justice as fairness without relying on a liberal or any other thick conception of the good. The organizing question Rawls poses is the following (PL: 4): "How is it possible for there to exist over time a just and stable society of free and equal citizens, who remain profoundly divided by reasonable religious, philosophical and moral doctrines?" Therefore, we begin with the idea that in democratic societies citizens come to have allegiance to different and incompatible metaphysical and moral beliefs. In some ways such a plurality of conceptions of the good is a practical outcome of the exercise by citizens of their democratic rights. In this sense, the claim of the fact of pluralism is an empirical generalization—the "inevitable outcome of free constitutions" (PL: 4). However, as the use of the word "inevitable" suggests, Rawls also thinks of the fact of pluralism as conceptually linked to the idea of democracy; a democracy in which there was no disagreement about what constituted the good—morally, metaphysically, and religiously—would suggest something sinister and decidedly undemocratic. Indeed, Rawls believes that agreement in a society on a single conception of the good would require the oppressive use of state power. Therefore, such an agreement is not possible in a functioning democracy where state power is exercised legitimately. If the two principles of justice are to govern the basic institutions of a democratic society they will have to be justified to citizens who hold very different views of the good.

The differences that Rawls has in mind, and the challenges that pluralism poses for the problem of justice, are severe and Rawls does not duck the difficulty of the problem. In reposing the question quoted above more "sharply" he questions (PL: xxxix): "How is it possible for those affirming a religious doctrine that is based on religious authority, for example, the Church or the Bible, also to hold a reasonable political conception that supports a just democratic regime?" The idea, then, is to defend justice as fairness as the correct account of justice for a democratic society in which citizens affirm not only a liberal conception of the good but also conceptions that hold very different notions of justification, truth, and morality.

FREESTANDING VIEWS

Rawls draws a distinction between a political conception of justice and "comprehensive doctrines." Comprehensive doctrines are thick, more or less articulate, conceptions of the good that form the basis of judgments concerning "what is of value in human life, the ideals of personal character, as well ideals of friendship and of familial and associational relationships, and much else that is to inform our conduct, and in the limit to our life as a whole" (PL: 13). Citizens are assumed to have some comprehensive doctrine that normatively informs their view of themselves and their world. Citizens who share comprehensive doctrines share a conception of the good and in a free society where differences in values are protected by democratic rights and liberties, citizens will also be divided by their comprehensive doctrines. They therefore owe allegiance to incompatible conceptions of what is good, what is worthwhile, and what is meaningful and purposeful in life.

It is obvious that principles of justice cannot be drawn from one particular comprehensive doctrine since that would raise the problem of stability; citizens who hold other comprehensive doctrines would lack the proper motivation to offer their free and willing support to such principles. The answer to the difficulty is to ground the principles in what Rawls calls a "freestanding view." Such a view is, in one way, distinct from citizens' particular comprehensive doctrines but, importantly, in another way, also embedded in them. A freestanding view is a *political* conception of justice that draws on shared ideas of the good but that does not affirm nor disaffirm any particular comprehensive doctrine (providing it is "reasonable"; an idea we will examine later). A political conception of justice is distinct from comprehensive doctrines in the following ways. First, the aim of a political conception is *practical* not "metaphysical." The aim is to find a way to organize the basic institutions of society so that they serve the cooperative purposes of citizens in a democratic society *in the right way.*

Second, the scope of moral concern of a political conception is narrower than a comprehensive doctrine. Whereas a comprehensive doctrine includes a conception of persons, beliefs about the good, and religious convictions—making it a "metaphysical" doctrine—a political conception includes only those values that are required to set out an account of justice based on citizens' shared values. A political conception therefore does include some notion of the good, but one that is shared, in a sense that is still to be explained. Finally, a political conception is *public.* In contrast, comprehensive doctrines, which are nonpublic, offer justifications and reasons for beliefs and convictions that appeal to others who share the same doctrine. For example, religious dietary beliefs are generally nonpublic in this way in that the reasons offered for not eating or eating certain foods have no grip on those who do not share the same comprehensive views. We will look much more closely at what Rawls means by "public" later. These three defining features of a political conception—its practical character, its limited scope, and the public reasons it offers—require substantial explanation and defense. We will attend to these explanations later. For now we should focus on the structural relationship that Rawls sets up between comprehensive doctrines and freestanding views.

There are two general problems that the idea of freestanding views is supposed to answer, namely, the problem of justification and the problem of motivation. A freestanding view should make "perspicuous to reason" what principles of justice ought to guide the basic institutions of society, and a freestanding view should motivate citizens to abide by these principles by engaging with what they have reason to value. The argument is that justice as fairness is such a freestanding view. Now a freestanding view that was entirely independent of all comprehensive doctrines would achieve neither of these aims. A comprehensive doctrine structures citizens' views of the world and alerts them to what counts as a good reason and to what matters about the world in which they live. Thus, a freestanding view needs to *overlap* with citizens' comprehensive doctrines to the extent that, from within their own comprehensive doctrines, citizens can see the point of the reasons offered by the freestanding view and to the extent that they will be moved to act on them. However, of course, the freestanding view cannot overlap so extensively with some comprehensive doctrines that others are excluded.

The clearest way to see this structural relationship is to picture comprehensive doctrines as a number of circles, each enclosed and distinct from each other. A freestanding view is a further circle that overlaps with all the other circles, being neither identical with nor entirely distinct from any of the (reasonable) comprehensive doctrines.

FREESTANDING VIEWS AS POLITICAL CONCEPTIONS

A freestanding view is not a comprehensive doctrine; a citizen could not adopt the freestanding view in place of her comprehensive doctrine. A freestanding view is limited to the political question of what principles should govern the basic structure of society. It does not, therefore, aim at providing a comprehensive perspective. From a structural standpoint one could have freestanding views concerning topics other than the political question of justice. Justice as fairness is a freestanding view that *is* a political conception of justice. To take the question of justice to require a political conception as a freestanding view is the central argument of the approach Rawls call "political liberalism." If we look back at *A Theory of Justice* we can see that a distinction needs to be drawn in that work between the political argument (in the sense of *political* we are using here) and the comprehensive argument. The former argument includes everything up to Rawls's answer to the question of stability where he relies on the Kantian notion of autonomy, which is, of course, part of a particular liberal comprehensive doctrine. For comprehensive liberals this is precisely the argument they want. Liberals want the political conception to engage with their comprehensive views in just this sort of way. Therefore, *A Theory of Justice* represents a special case of an argument for a political conception of justice directed at comprehensive liberals. Therefore, the "error" in *A Theory of Justice* is just an error of perspective not of argument. What needs correction is how we view the relationship between the political and the comprehensive elements in the text. *Political Liberalism* attempts to shift our perspective. In so doing, it also changes the way we read and understand *A Theory of Justice.*

The contrast between a political conception of justice and a metaphysical view is that the former is freestanding and the latter takes up the question of justice entirely from within a comprehensive doctrine. A metaphysical conception of justice, for example, a liberal or a religious view, is a moral one; it states what ought to be the case. A political conception is also a moral view. It is, however, a moral view that draws on a spread of other moral views. The difference is not that a political conception is not a moral view whereas a metaphysical view is such a view, but that the *scope* of these views is different. A political conception applies shared moral values and norms to "a specific kind of subject"; the basic structure of society. It is clear that political liberalism is not an attempt to escape the level of the normative and found principles of justice on rationality alone. However, if the appeal of the principles is not to citizens' rationality (their sense of self-interest) but to their moral commitments, then two pressing questions emerge. First, what is the basis for the claim that there is an overlap in moral perspectives between citizens? Second, what of those citizens, for surely there must be some, whose moral views do not overlap with others?

The first question is answered by Rawls when he says that "justice as fairness starts from within a certain political tradition" (PL: 14). It draws on ideas embedded in the history and traditions of a democratic society. The idea is that there is a background of moral ideas against which comprehensive doctrines in a democratic society are located. In their different ways, comprehensive doctrines draw on, respond to, and are molded by, these ideas. The moral value of equality, for example, is an idea implicit in the culture and tradition of democratic societies but it is taken up in different ways by comprehensive doctrines. Comprehensive liberals might understand the value of equality in terms of autonomous agency whereas a Christian religious doctrine might understand equality in terms of equality in the eyes of God. What matters, though, is that the moral value of equality in a very broad sense is one that forms part of the backdrop of citizens' self-understanding in a democratic society. It is these sorts of ideas that a political conception will draw on to form the basis of an argument for principles of justice. More particularly justice as fairness, as a political conception, relies on the idea of equality as part of its argument for the two principles. Two related issues arise at this juncture, although a full discussion of them has to wait until later. First, are the shared moral norms substantive enough to bear the justificatory and motivational weight that a political conception places on them? For instance, in our example above, it might be argued that the idea of equality that Christians and liberals share is in fact so different that the common designation "equality" is misleading, their understandings being too far distant from one another. Second, Rawls requires both differences among comprehensive doctrines and similarities in order to anchor the background ideas that will form the basis of a political conception of the good suited to justice as fairness. A society that was fundamentally divided in its traditions and culture would, presumably, lack the requisite background of shared fundamental ideas needed for agreement on a just society. The kinds of democratic societies that Rawls has in mind, then, are those that have the right sort of tradition and culture.

This leads us to the second question asked above. This concerns citizens who subscribe to comprehensive doctrines that do not share these fundamental political values and thus that do not have the requisite normative resources for participating in a consensus on principles of justice for their society. In the first place, this is not a problem for a democratic society providing such citizens are a minority, providing a democratic state is "willingly and freely supported by at least a substantial majority of its politically active citizens" (PL: 38). The question is one of the limits of toleration, and the sorts of considerations advanced in our earlier discussion of toleration apply here, too. However, the question does alert us to the need to distinguish between comprehensive doctrines that can and cannot form part of an agreement on principles of justice, and the need for a determination of the criteria for making this distinction. The basis for these criteria is the idea of reasonableness, which will be defined further below. For now though, we can say that persons and, more generally, comprehensive doctrines that are unreasonable lack the required moral resources to be part of a just constitutional democracy.

In conclusion, we can say that a political conception of the good (a freestanding view) seeks to ground itself on the shared values and norms of reasonable comprehensive doctrines. It does so by offering a justification for principles of justice that is situated in a political tradition that forms a common background to these doctrines, and that offers a moral vision that has a prescriptive grip on citizens, thus providing the basis of a shared, albeit thin, conception of the good.

2. The Justification of the Principles Reconsidered

Rawls offers an account of justification in three connected parts. First, a political conception of justice is constructed relying on and grounded in political values. Justice as fairness is an example of such a justification. He calls such a construction a *pro tanto* justification. Second, justification requires that the political conception of justice is properly connected to and is embedded in citizens' comprehensive doctrines in what he calls an *overlapping consensus*. Finally, the third level of justification demands that the political conception, grounded in a reasonable overlapping consensus, forms the basis for a public deliberative framework he calls the "idea of public reason." We will examine each of these levels of justification in turn.

Political Constructivism

In our earlier discussion of the justification of the two principles in *A Theory of Justice* we focused on the idea of reflective equilibrium as the source of justification for these principles. Wide reflective equilibrium remains the justificatory standard in *Political Liberalism*; however, Rawls offers a much more elaborate account of how this can be achieved. This new account is partly a clarification and expansion of the method of reasoning used in support of the two principles, and partly it is a response to the challenges posed by the recognition of a plurality of conceptions of the good in democratic societies. This new theory of justification is "political constructivism." *A Theory of Justice* exemplifies political constructivism at work once we understand its aims as political rather than metaphysical.

In general, political constructivism argues that the principles of justice that govern the basic institutions of society are derived from a procedure of construction. The principles are constructed or assembled through a procedure that takes a particular conception of persons and society as it material. The combination of this material (conceptions of persons and society) and the procedure yields particular principles. The abstractness of this idea is much easier to grasp if we look back at the original position and see how political constructivism actually works out in the case of justice as fairness. We should remember that justice as fairness is an instance of the more general approach of political constructivism, and different conceptions of persons and/or society will likely yield different principles. A second general point that Rawls is keen to make clear is that political constructivism has practical and not epistemological aims. By this he means that political constructivism is limited not only in the scope of the justification it offers—applying only to the limited question of justice and not to morality as a whole—it is also limited in its aim. It seeks not truth but practical agreement. Truth is the aim of the natural and social sciences, and it is also the claim of many comprehensive doctrines for their moral and metaphysical beliefs.

Political constructivism, as we will see later in this section, does not lay claim to the truth of the principles it constructs, although citizens are free to take the principles as true insofar as they resonate with beliefs that they take to be true from the perspective of their comprehensive doctrines. The aim of political constructivism is the practical justification of principles governing the basic institutions, that is, deriving principles that citizens have reason to acknowledge and abide by. Rawls does not mean by a practical agreement a mere *modus vivendi* agreement, that is, a balance of forces or a purely strategic compromise. He will argue that a practical agreement, in the sense he understands it, is a moral agreement of limited scope, but one anchored in the separate reasonable comprehensive doctrines of citizens.

In summary, political constructivism specifies a procedure for deriving principles of justice and has a practical aim or purpose. We might say, political constructivism is a theory of justification that is practical and procedural. In the following discussion we will unpack the idea of political constructivism by looking at its idea of objectivity.

OBJECTIVITY

Objectivity is the mark of a justified political claim. Thus political constructivism seeks to occupy an objective point of view from which we, the readers, will comprehend the justificatory claim made on behalf of the principles. As we noted in our discussion of reflective equilibrium, this objective point of view is contrasted with the private, subjective point of view of citizens. To be justified in one's claims is to have reasons that, in principle, can appeal to others and that they could accept as their own reasons. To say that one's judgments are true is a typical way to claim to an objective perspective. Truth judgments are, in principle, available to anyone. Since a proposition is true independently of any subjective belief, the perspective that truth offers is a "view from nowhere." However, as we saw above, political liberalism does not have an epistemological aim and so it does not say that the principles it constructs are true. It therefore surrenders that source of objectivity. Instead of truth as the guiding concept for the objective point view, Rawls's conception of objectivity establishes "a public framework of thought" (PL: 110).

Citizens thus enter into such a framework and are guided in their deliberations and discussions. They are shifted from their private and particular points of view towards a shared understanding. Therefore, given the practical aim of political constructivism, a shared understanding stands as the standard of objectivity for the principles. Of course, this says far too little. What does having "a shared understanding" mean? What is meant by a "public framework" and how are citizens' deliberations guided by it? These questions are addressed below. What matters at this point is that Rawls deploys a particular conception of objectivity that has the task of providing the necessary justificatory foundation for the two principles. The standard of objectivity is not truth but the deliverances of practical reason aimed at an agreement on principles of justice. In summary Rawls says (PL: 119):

> Political convictions (which are also of course, moral convictions) are objective—actually founded on an order of reasons—if reasonable and rational persons, who are sufficiently intelligent and conscientious in exercising their powers of practical reason, and whose reasoning exhibits none of the familiar defects of reasoning, would eventually endorse those convictions, or sufficiently narrow their differences about them, provided that these persons know the relevant facts and have sufficiently surveyed the grounds that bear on the matter under conditions favorable to due reflection.

METHOD

We are already familiar with an application of the method of political constructivism; the reasoning in the original position is an instance of it. Four elements, identified in our earlier discussion, are required by the constructivist procedure: (a) a conception of the person, (b) a conception of society, (c) a structure or framework that guides our reasoning (or better, that models an ideal of practical reason), and (d) an argument that links these three elements to a set of principles that constitute objective norms to order the basic structure. Justice as fairness conceives of persons as rational and reasonable and society as well-ordered. The original position is, as we have said, a device for perspicuously demonstrating the deliberations of practical reason when applied to persons and society so conceived. It is aimed at agreement on principles of justice. Rawls sums up the constructivist method by saying (PL: 104):

> not everything is constructed; we must have some material, as it were, from which to begin. In a more literal sense, only the substantive principles specifying the content of political right and justice are con-

> structed. The procedure itself is simply laid out using as starting points the basic conceptions of society and persons, the principles of practical reason, and the public role of a political conception of justice.

Our political judgments (as citizens of a constitutional democracy) concerning justice are, therefore, well-founded when they are in agreement with what the contractors would agree to. They are not well-founded otherwise. Moreover, the original position tells us why our judgments are right when they are, and conversely, why they are wrong when are they are not. Finally, if our considered judgments are in conflict with the principles, then, either the initial situation has a faulty conception of persons or society (or both), or displays faulty reasoning. It is, of course, unnecessary here to recount the structure of the original position or rehearse the reasoning of the contractors since we have covered this ground in part one. Rawls does however add to his account the idea of the "reasonable" that has important consequences.

REASONABLENESS

When we set out the original position the idea of the reasonable was defined in terms of the contractors having a "sense of justice." This meant that the contractors were willing to enter into agreements with others and to abide by the agreements they made (providing others did as well). This idea of reasonableness was contrasted with the idea of the rational. The latter specifies that the contractors had a conception of the good and that they chose the most efficient means for realizing this conception. This was enough, it seemed, for the contractors to have sufficient motivation to enter into agreement with one another and to have confidence in the stability of the agreement reached. In later work, and in particular in *Political Liberalism*, Rawls makes clear the priority of the reasonable; the reasonable "subordinates" the rational in the sense that the willingness to keep one's agreements, under normal conditions, is a stronger tendency than the tendency to seek the satisfaction of one's own conception of the good at the expense of others. Furthermore, persons have a "higher-order" interest in realizing their powers of rationality and reasonableness. This is an important clarification because it is not enough that persons have particular capacities for rationality and reasonableness. It is essential that they have an interest in realizing them, since otherwise these capacities will not be effective in the way Rawls's theory requires. While these clarifications are important, the most significant change in the account of reasonableness that Rawls proposes in *Political Liberalism* is an adjustment required by the move from a comprehensive view to a political one, and so is worthy of some detailed attention here.

The Burdens of Judgment

Reasonable people *and* the reasonable comprehensive doctrines they subscribe to seek justice. They search for principles that all can agree to and sincerely abide by, even if in so doing some measure of sacrifice is required. So far such a view of reasonableness is compatible with both epistemological and practical aims. However, given the fact of a plurality of conceptions of the good (alternative and incompatible beliefs concerning morality, religion, and metaphysics) it is obvious that citizens who are reasonable (they have an active sense of justice) will nonetheless disagree with one another about the good. Rawls distinguishes between reasonable and unreasonable disagreement. The latter conflicts arise from the usual defects of practical reasoning such as general prejudice, egoism, racism, deficiencies of reason, purposeful ignorance, and so on. However, once we clear away such defects it's still possible that citizens will disagree. In fact, given pluralism, we should expect them to disagree in a democratic society. The issue for Rawls is not how to overcome such conflicts (although the extent to which they can be overcome is important and the narrowing of disagreements is also important), but rather what *attitude* citizens take to the disagreements they encounter.

Differences between people on matters concerning theoretical reason demand the stern attitude of the truth seeker; after all, the presumption of theoretical reason (in the natural and social sciences particularly but also in many moral and theological sciences) is that there is some truth to be uncovered, some fact or best theory that explains the facts. It would be a failure of theoretical reason to be indifferent to the truth and to tolerate (in an intellectual sense) differences between people (which is not to say that every theoretical question can be answered and that a certain humility in the face of the world is not sometimes called for). However, for practical reason, with its nonepistemological aims, the required attitude is different. Since there is no transcendent realm of fact or best theory to explain matters, practical reasoners, insofar as they are reasonable, strike an attitude of diffidence towards their own and others' claims. They acknowledge and recognize the distinction between theoretical and practical reason, and they adopt the attitude appropriate to each form of reason. Overall, Rawls says (PL: 58): "Many of our most important judgments are made under conditions where it is not to be expected that conscientious persons with full powers of reason, even after free discussion, will all arrive at the same conclusion." Rawls illustrates this attitude of diffidence by pointing to six instances where such an attitude is appropriate (PL: 56–57). Among these are situations in which the evidence (gathered by theoretical reason and used in support of moral or religious claims) is complex "and thus hard to assess and evaluate." Differences in how we weigh evidence, the vagueness of our concepts, the narrowness of our perspectives, differences of "kinds of normative considerations of different force on both sides of an issue," and the fact that we sometimes have to choose between "cherished values" we wish to realize in the "limited social space" available to us. Collectively, instances of persistent disagreement are what Rawls describes as the "burdens of judgment." We are called on to make judgments in the practical sphere where our confidence in their rightness is, of necessity, limited. Reasonable people, in Rawls's account, accept and understand this. The attitude called up by the burdens of judgment is, of course, directed not only at the judgments of others but also at one's own judgments.

To be unreasonable then is to suppose that the burdens of judgment do not apply to one's own comprehensive beliefs *when these beliefs are articulated and presented in deliberations concerning justice and the political values in general.* The qualification italicized in the previous sentence is required because when in the comprehensive mode Rawls allows that one's attitude to one's moral and religious beliefs may be different. For example, in the comprehensive mode a religious person may well regard her belief in the existence of a deity to be true in the most robust sense of being true. However, in the political mode where her aim is securing a consensus on principles of justice, the reasonable religious person adopts the practical attitude necessitated by her acknowledgment of the burdens of judgment. By contrast a secular liberal may accept the burdens of judgment with regard to her comprehensive beliefs as well as her political ones although, of course, a secular liberal may regard her liberal political beliefs as being true in the strongest sense. Therefore, reasonableness does *not* signify diffidence towards one's most treasured comprehensive beliefs. In fact, Rawls's argument here seems compatible with the most earnest and devout of religious and metaphysical beliefs. What marks out reasonableness here is not the strength or attachment to a belief but the appropriateness of the attitude adopted in the two spheres of the political and the comprehensive.

At this juncture a common criticism of Rawls is this bifurcation between comprehensive and political attitudes. It has been argued that citizens cannot be expected to adopt such a schizophrenic attitude towards their beliefs; one either does or does not believe something. However, we should distinguish the empirical claim that people can or cannot adopt the political attitude towards their beliefs from the normative claim that they ought to. The anecdotal empirical evidence suggests that some people can and others cannot distinguish the political and the comprehensive mode with regard to their cherished beliefs. This does not bear on Rawls's *normative* argument. Rawls asks what must be the case for justice in pluralistic democratic societies to be possible (this is a transcendental question). Reasonableness, including the acknowledgment of the burdens of judgment, is part of his answer. Citizens have to be reasonable if they are to live in a society approaching justice.

A further argument against Rawls may be made from the communitarian point of view. It will be said that this dissociation between a person and her beliefs demanded by the political attitude reveals the individualistic bias in Rawls's account of justice. A theory that emphasized community rather than individuals would show how individuals' beliefs and self-conception were tied to their historical and communal circumstances, and therefore an individual could not differentiate herself from her beliefs. The Rawlsian response to this would be no different than the arguments explained and assessed in the section on communitarian criticisms of *A Theory of Justice*, and so it is unnecessary to repeat them here.

Finally, it is important to point out that the attitude of diffidence underlying the acceptance of the burdens of judgment is not one of skepticism. A theory of justice that required citizens to be skeptical about their own beliefs would be unacceptable normatively, and extremely doubtful as an empirical possibility. Reasonable citizens can take their beliefs to be true and certain in the comprehensive mode. Furthermore, they are not disbelieving or doubtful of their beliefs in the political mode; they just do not press their beliefs as truthful or certain *trumps* in their deliberations with others on questions of justice. For example, one can take very seriously one's belief that all human life, including potential human life, is sacred without imposing one's belief on others and also recognize that reason and evidence falls short in providing a decisive argument in one's favor. Reasonable citizens are therefore tolerant citizens and "these burdens of judgment are of first significance for a democratic idea of toleration" (PL: 58).

The burdens of judgment are therefore at the center of Rawls's argument for political liberalism, especially insofar as they define and limit the kinds of reasons and arguments citizens can put forward in political deliberation. How this unfolds will be clearer when we turn to the explanation of what Rawls means by public reasons later. First though, we need to say something briefly about what counts as a reasonable comprehensive doctrine and say something more substantial about the idea of an overlapping consensus.

Reasonable Comprehensive Doctrines

We are now in a position to say what Rawls means by a *reasonable* comprehensive doctrine. This is clearly an important task since only reasonable comprehensive doctrines can be part of an overlapping consensus on principles of justice. The idea of reasonableness is therefore an exclusionary criterion. It marks off some conceptions of the good as ineligible to participate in citizens' deliberations concerning the structure of society's fundamental institutions and the "benefits and burdens" that flow from them.

Simply put, reasonable comprehensive doctrines are those doctrines that reasonable citizens affirm. Citizens who seek agreement on the basic questions of justice, who have a sense of justice and are thus willing to keep to the agreements they make, and who acknowledge the burdens of judgment affirm doctrines that are reasonable. There are, however, some additional markers of reasonable comprehensive doctrines. A reasonable comprehensive doctrine is general insofar as "it covers the major religious, philosophical, and moral aspects of human life in a more or less consistent and coherent manner" (PL: 59). Second, it orders and resolves conflicts between values, and finally, "it belongs to, or draws upon, a tradition of thought and doctrine" (PL: 59). The first and second markers are familiar to us from our earlier account of what Rawls means by having a conception of the good. The contractors take themselves to have moral, religious, and metaphysical commitments in the original position, and citizens have a corresponding, more or less articulated, set of beliefs, values, and attitudes. The third marker is an important addition; it signals that reasonable comprehensive doctrines are typically embedded in a democratic society's intellectual past. They are organic in this sense, emerging from traditions within a society that have achieved the allegiance of other citizens. By being rooted in the traditions of society, reasonable comprehensive doctrines already share a collective history, even if their responses and attitudes towards it are very different. This fact will be significant when we look at the possibilities for realizing an overlapping consensus in the next subsection. The third marker also signifies that reasonable comprehensive doctrines are plastic and so are not dogmas but rather they change with time and circumstance.

Fundamentalist religious doctrines that demand and expect the state to promote their particular conception of the good are unreasonable in Rawls's sense. Their unreasonableness is most clearly captured in their willingness to use the state's coercive power to enforce their beliefs on unbelieving citizens. However, we should tread carefully here because Rawls is not arguing that unreasonable comprehensive doctrines should be suppressed in a democratic society. Again, unreasonable doctrines should be tolerated provided that they pose no real threat to the basic freedoms and liberties of other citizens. This is the standard of Rawls's notion of democratic toleration, as we have seen. Of course, this abstract standard is merely a guide to particular cases and it is difficult to establish the precise point at which basic freedoms are genuinely in danger. Additionally, not all questions about unreasonable comprehensive doctrines can be settled even in the abstract by Rawlsian standards of toleration, especially where basic liberties conflict as they do. For example, in cases where children of parents who affirm unreasonable doctrines claim the right to educate their children in the values of that doctrine.

The Overlapping Consensus

We are now in a position to pull together the threads of this discussion so far and offer an account of how Rawls explains the possibility of agreement on principles of justice in a democratic society marked by pluralism. This is the second step in Rawls's account of justification. There are two sides to this argument that we should keep firmly in view; the role of the overlapping consensus in grounding the justification for the principles, and the role of the overlapping consensus in providing the basis for the motivation for citizens to abide by the principles they agree to. It is the former concern that we will discuss further. The latter motivational concern will be addressed when we turn to the relation between the right and the good under political liberalism.

The main idea of political liberalism is that agreement is possible on a set of values in a pluralistic society. This set of values is a shared subset of the comprehensive values each citizen affirms from the perspective of her comprehensive doctrine. In other words, a consensus is possible between opposed comprehensive doctrines that share some subset of common values, that is, the political values, and this is what Rawls describes as an *overlapping consensus.* Therefore an overlapping consensus is only possible between reasonable comprehensive doctrines and is not a solution to what we might call the problem of radical pluralism. The latter would be a situation in which citizens with allegiance to unreasonable comprehensive doctrines formed a significant part of society (either in terms of numbers or power and influence). The political values that form the basis of a consensus for a democratic society are those that are represented in the original position in the description of the contractors and the account of a well-ordered society. Therefore, in a constitutional democracy, according to Rawls, a consensus is possible between citizens who affirm the values of freedom and equality, who have a sense of justice, and who understand their society as place of reciprocity and mutual advantage. There are four main points to be made about Rawls's account of the overlapping consensus.

First, citizens disagree about fundamental values such as the meaning and purpose of life, the importance of religion, and so on. They *do* agree on the political values. It is not enough though that the political values are shared—they must also *outweigh* the other important values contained within the comprehensive doctrine. Thus, the political values must not only be present as values but also have priority. In fact, Rawls says the political values must be regarded as "very great values" that govern "the very groundwork of our existence" and that constitute the "fundamental terms of political and social cooperation" (PL: 139). In summary, reasonable comprehensive doctrines are those that have *both* the political values required for a constitutional democracy and which affirm these values to the greatest degree. Citizens' conceptions of the good in a democratic society are therefore limited further by this requirement.

We have emphasized that for Rawls political values are moral values, although they concern and cover a smaller range than the array of moral values that typically constitute a comprehensive doctrine. For this reason an overlapping consensus is a moral agreement. This point is vital to Rawls's project. An agreement that is strategic rather than moral is one based on *interests*. Citizens who come to a strategic agreement commit themselves to a cooperative venture in order to secure and further their own, or their group's, interests. The agreement is a *modus vivendi* agreement that has prudential rather than moral value for the participants. Now, *modus vivendi* agreements are fundamentally unstable. They last as long as the participants believe that they profit from the arrangement. Since what Rawls is seeking is stability it is clear that it would be a confusion to regard an overlapping consensus as a mere alignment of strategic interests. The second main point then is that the justification of an overlapping consensus rests on moral grounds and not only on the interests of the parties to the agreement; it is not a *modus vivendi* agreement.

Third, the source of the shared political values is each citizen's comprehensive doctrine and so although citizens agree on the political values they do not (necessarily) agree on the moral justification of them. Citizens can, and most likely do, have very *different* moral reasons for affirming the *same* political values. For instance, a Christian might have a very different moral justification for the value of equality than a secular liberal. The former might base her argument for political equality on the equality we share in the "eyes of God," whereas the secular liberal might base her argument on a Kantian account of human dignity. Citizens therefore can have different reasons for affirming the same values.

Finally, as we have already seen, the political conception of justice, grounded in the shared subset of political values that all reasonable citizens share, neither asserts nor denies the truth of comprehensive doctrines (PL: 153). In the political mode citizens recognize the burdens of judgment, they acknowledge the requirements of public reason, and so on, and refrain from judging reasonable comprehensive doctrines. This is not skepticism about the source and justification of political values. In the comprehensive mode citizens may regard the political conception of justice as true, although they leave this assertive epistemic judgment aside when they change over to the political mode.

In conclusion, the idea, as Rawls states it, is to find a "concordant fit between the political conception and the comprehensive views together with the public recognition of the great values of the political virtues" (PL: 171). Of course, there are, potentially, many possible "concordant fits" between sets of comprehensive doctrines and sets of political conceptions. The idea of the overlapping consensus is structural in nature; it provides a form in which pluralities of comprehensive doctrines can find a morally-based agreement on a political conception of justice. In addition to setting out this structure, Rawls also provides the content for a *particular* overlapping consensus, the theory of justice as fairness. The content of this latter consensus is provided by the political conception of justice worked out through the original position for citizens of a constitutional democracy. The claim that an overlapping consensus is a morally-based agreement and how this claim addresses the problem of motivation will be examined later.

Public Reason

Political constructivism is a method of justification that, Rawls argues, grounds justice as fairness. The theory of the overlapping consensus explains how a political conception of justice, a *pro tanto* justification, comes to be embedded in the reasonable comprehensive doctrines of citizens and can thus be appropriately connected to their conceptions of the good. The idea of public reason raises the question of justification again, but in a different way. Whereas political constructivism is a narrow philosophical theory about how to ground normative political claims, and the idea of an overlapping consensus tells us how citizens come to have allegiance to political principles, the idea of public reason is a much wider argument concerning what is practically required for the very possibility of democratic society as an ongoing enterprise. Stability requires more than a political conception of justice about which there is consensus. It also requires an account of how citizens conduct a political life in common. The shared political values and ideals need to be animated through a discursive framework that allows for genuine democratic deliberation between citizens on matters of great political importance. Stability therefore requires a dynamic account of deliberation that permits citizens to conduct their political lives "before others without criticizing and rejecting their deepest religious and philosophical commitments" (PL: 390). Thus, the argument for the idea of public reason is both practical and transcendental; it tells us what citizens need to *do* in their reasoning to come to a stable agreement on political questions and it arrives at this practical conclusion through asking what makes democratic society under conditions of a reasonable pluralism *possible*. Rawls's theory of public reason can be considered the culminating moment of his theory of domestic justice. It draws together and relies on the multitude of distinctions we have already worked through and brings new insights into the requirements and implications of political liberalism. If the idea of the original position was the great moment of philosophical originality at the beginning of Rawls's career, the idea of public reason is a great moment of philosophical synthesis towards its end. Rawls's account of public reason developed slowly and required numerous changes and adjustments. He was unsatisfied with his first account in the original edition of *Political Liberalism* and wrote a new introduction to the paperback edition largely devoted to reworking his ideas about public reason. In 1997 he revised his arguments again in an essay called "The Idea of Public Reason Revisited," which was added to later editions of *Political Liberalism* and included in *The Law of Peoples*.

The main idea is that political questions in a constitutional democracy are (or should be) settled by appeal to "public" reasons. We might think of this as asserting that citizens in democratic societies have a form of reasoning that is collective and inclusive. In contrast, nondemocratic societies have only the private reasons of individuals and groups and therefore the reasons offered in such a society are exclusive and not ones that any member of society could, in principle, call their own. Citizens of a democratic society also have private reasons, of course, and these are lodged in their comprehensive doctrines. These private reasons are either the reasons of individuals or the reasons of associations like churches, clubs, and universities. What such citizens have in addition though is a capacity for collective reason and suitable institutionalized forums for the exercise of this reason. As we will see the exercise of public reason is a legal requirement of some citizens and the moral duty of all citizens in some circumstances.

This is the first definition of what is public about public reasoning. It is the reasoning of a democratic public when considering fundamental questions of social justice. Second, public reason is aimed at answering a particular question, namely, what are the principles that ought to govern the basic institutions of society. Public reason thus aims at revealing the public good. Third, public reason is reasons shared, it has a public rather than private purpose, and so the reasons offered to others have the character of being designed to illicit the uncoerced and nonstrategic consent of all citizens. None of these ideas are new to us. We have met them all before in one form or another earlier in this book. However, they are now brought together under the single concept of public reason.

We can elaborate on the three definitions of public reason Rawls has given us. Public reason is a discursive activity that democratic citizens engage in when they aim to persuade one another on questions to do with how power ought to be exercised in their society. In a democracy power is, ideally, wielded by the people, the collectivity of citizens. The procedures by which citizens make decisions are embodied in institutions such as a parliament, a legal system, and an election process. In each of these institutions citizens offer and receive opinions, ideas, and reasons that form the basis of decisions that fundamentally affect the life prospects of some and sometimes all citizens. This discursive activity is thus crucial to the legitimacy of actions undertaken through democratic institutions. A public reason thus grounds the legitimacy of the use of power in a democracy. What would be the characteristics of such a reason? To begin with we might think that only the unanimous consent of all those affected by a decision could ultimately ground the legitimacy of the exercise of power in a democracy; if we all agree then we all are, in a sense, both those who exercise power as well as those on whom it is exercised. If we give ourselves a rule, then we are not ruled by others. Citizens in an ideal democracy give rules to themselves and abide by these rules not from fear of tyranny and not from habit and custom. They are free from the arbitrary exercise of power of others. However, as we will see below, the ideal of unanimous consent and self-given reasons is not an ideal that Rawls affirms as the basis for legitimacy in a constitutional democracy.

We know already that Rawls expects, in a fully just democracy, only agreement on the political values and not agreement on all questions of metaphysical, moral, and religious values. The political values animate the institutions of a democracy but, even in a just democracy, and especially in democracies that are not fully just, there will be differences in the understanding, interpreting, and ordering of these values. While agreement and consent are the aims of political discourse, democracies have to have a way of practicing disagreement and dissent. The idea of public reason is to reach for agreement while acknowledging and accommodating disagreement. A public reason does this by offering considerations that others could, in principle, accept. In other words, it makes an appeal to ideas and values that other citizens have reason to agree with. This is what makes a reason public rather than private. A private reason (individual or associational) is one that has a persuasive grip only on those who already subscribe to a particular way of thinking about the matter at hand. For example, offering a reason based solely on a religious conviction to a fellow citizen who does not share your religious beliefs is not a reason one could reasonably expect her to consent to. It is a private rather than a public reason. The reasons that structure citizens' comprehensive doctrines are private in this sense and form the background culture of society. Reasons that are persuasive only to those who share one's comprehensive doctrine, or some parts of it, do not aim at agreement at the political level and so are not public. We need to be cautious because the relationship between public and private reasons, between the background culture of reasonable comprehensive doctrines and the public political culture of society, is complex as we will see below. But for now, we need only to mark a basic conceptual difference and recognize the aim of public reason.

A reason that others could reasonably accept (or not reasonably reject) is not a guarantee that they will do so, of course. There may be "interference" from a person's comprehensive doctrine that prevents her from recognizing the force of the political reason offered or there may be other, more compelling, public reasons available that the person believes trumps the reason offered. Furthermore, the public character of a reason is only a formal feature and its being a public reason does not mean that it is a good reason. There will be bad reasons that are also public reasons. To use an extreme example, someone might argue on the basis of freedom (a public, political value) that children ought to be granted gun licenses. Since freedom, in a constitutional democracy is shared political value and not one rooted in a particular comprehensive doctrine it can be part, formally, of a public reason since other citizens could accept freedom as a sound basis for accepting and agreeing to the proposition. I assume readers will agree with me that it is not a good idea for children to have guns and so this is a bad, although public, reason. We will examine a number of examples of public reasons and reasoning later on.

Public reasoning is therefore a legitimizing discursive activity that is characterized by the formal feature of appealing only to reasons that all citizens *could* reasonably accept (or not reject). This does not, of course, meet the standard of unanimous consent we spoke of earlier. If, ideally, all decisions that affect citizens are taken with regard to only public reasons it does not follow that all citizens have fully consented to these decisions; after all, they might have rejected the public reasons offered (perhaps rightly). However, the standard of unanimous consent is questionable not only practically where it approaches an empirical impossibility, but also conceptually. If we understand modern democratic societies as inevitably pluralistic in the way Rawls does, then either we must abandon the idea of political legitimacy altogether or we have to explore alternatives. The idea of public reason is just such an alternative. As is typical with Rawls's philosophy, it weaves a path between the impossible standard of unanimous consent and the subjective relativity of legitimacy as mere ideology.

An appropriate public political discourse in a democracy is characterized in one sense by the formal features described above, but it is also characterized by a particular *attitude* among citizens towards their fellow citizens in their political relations. This is an attitude of what Rawls calls "civic friendship." Again, this is not a new idea. The contractors in the original position viewed society as a place of ***mutual*** advantage and more recently we have emphasized the importance of the notion of reciprocity among citizens in a democracy. The idea of civic friendship pushes further the emphasis on mutuality and reciprocity in the ideal of democratic citizenship. Citizens are not disinterested in how their fellow citizens fare and are not disinterested in how their own decisions affect others in their society. The use of public reasons as the basis of political discourse is part of an attitude of friendship since such reasons attempt to illicit the genuine consent of others. This acknowledges the other as a political equal and deserving of respect. Equality and respect are of course the basis of any kind of friendship.

Rawls is speaking of *civic* friendship and not a generalized fellow-feeling among citizens. It is in the political arena where we meet as citizens to decide issues of basic justice that we adopt the attitude of friendship towards each other. It is as political actors that we are friends and acknowledge our reciprocal and mutual relations as well as our equality and claims to respect. Outside of our political lives our relations of friendship and reciprocity are informed by our comprehensive doctrines and conceptions of the good and so our relations with others outside of the political arena will be as extensive and as deep as our comprehensive doctrine allows and demands.

We have identified the formal discursive characteristics of public reason and we have identified the attitude of civic friendship that informs public political discourse. We now need to specify exactly the scope of public reason by saying which citizens are obligated to use public reasons and in what circumstances. Once this task is accomplished we need to say more exactly how Rawls both distinguishes public reasons from the background culture and specify more clearly the relations between these two spheres.

The requirement to reason publicly applies to discussions about fundamental issues of political values and the public good when these are conducted in what Rawls calls "the public political forum" (LoP: 133). He has in mind three sites of discourse: (1) the discourse of judges in a supreme court, (2) the discourse of government officials and legislators, and (3) the discourse of candidates for public office. Officials in these forums are obligated to justify their decisions and proposals by offering reasons that they sincerely believe are reasonable and thus reasons that others could accept. Individual citizens are not obligated to discuss political issues with each other in this restricted way. However, Rawls does say that when citizens vote in elections they should make choices and decisions *as if* they were legislators. In other words, Rawls sees democratic voting not as a means of expressing and aggregating citizens' private preferences but as a public political act in which citizens rise above private preference and consider the public good.

Rawls has distinguished between the background culture of comprehensive doctrines and the forums of political discourse. We have also made a fairly sharp distinction in line with this between public reason and private reason. However, Rawls argues that in practice such a sharp distinction is neither possible or, in some cases, desirable. Therefore, we can distinguish between a narrow or exclusive understanding of public reason and what Rawls calls the wide view. The former understanding seeks to keep the distinction between public reason and private reason sharp. It does so to exclude reasoning and discourse that is grounded in comprehensive doctrines from "contaminating" the public political discourse. Where considerations that belong to comprehensive doctrines are used to make and justify decisions that result in the use of the coercive power of the state this is regarded as a failure *always*. Rawls comes to reject this view as too restrictive on public discourse. He argues that insight into injustices and the vocabulary to describe these injustices may, *to begin with*, only be available in the language of a citizen's comprehensive doctrine. For example, he believes that this was the case for some of the activists of the American civil rights movement. What matters, he says, is that "in due course proper political reasons . . . are presented" (LoP: 152). This concession he calls the "Proviso." The proviso thus sets the aim of political discourse towards the ideal of public reason but recognizes that people grasp and interpret the world first through the lens of their comprehensive doctrines. Furthermore, Rawls says it is sometimes appropriate to introduce comprehensive views into the public discourse to show citizens how their private views can, in fact, support and ground democratic political values. In other words, there might be a perfectly reasonable *political* argument to support a citizen's view which she fails to see for herself. Showing her this connection requires bringing comprehensive views into the public arena.

The wide view of public reason erases the sharp boundary between the public and the private in political discourse. It sets a looser standard than the narrow view. However, Rawls is clear that different forums of political discourse should cleave to tighter standards than others. Thus, a supreme court should be an exemplar of public reason making the clearest distinction between public reason and comprehensive views. Political activists challenging perceived injustices have a much looser obligation. Between these stand the legislators and candidates and voters. While the proviso permits the employment of comprehensive views in public discourse it does not exempt discussants from being challenged to explain the connection between their comprehensive views and the political values and the demand for reasonable agreement. The distinction between the public and the private is thus always kept in sight on the wide view but not always imposed. The cost in conceptual clarity of the move to the wide view is paid for with a more plausible practical understanding of how democratic politics works.

Before we move on to look at Rawls's response to some challenges to the idea of public reason we should briefly consider some examples of public reasoning. Public reason neither settles questions in advance nor sets the agenda for what kinds of question can arise. Some questions seem easy to answer from the perspective of public reason such as the equal rights of all citizens to vote. The political values of freedom and equality obviously apply and the case for voting rights can easily be made. However, a universal franchise is a relatively recent feature of liberal societies and the argument for enfranchising all men first and then women only came after much public debate and struggle. What is clear to us now as democratic citizens was not so clear to our grandfathers and grandmothers. Our present struggles over the role of religion in schools, gay marriage, and abortion are all open questions as far as the idea of public reason is concerned. The crucial question is whether a reasonable political argument can be made. For example, allowing pupils to pray in school might be argued for on the basis of their freedom of religious expression. The political value of freedom is therefore the ground for this argument. However, to argue that pupils should pray because of the revealed truth of a particular religion would not count as reasonable since it rests exclusively on private reasons. The arguments of the Massachusetts

Supreme Court allowing gay marriage in the state were likewise couched in the language of the political value of equality for all citizens. Arguments against gay marriage that claim that children need heterosexual parents for their healthy development are also arguments couched in political values. In this case the appeal is to the right of children to become fully capable citizens and members of society. This emphasizes the points made earlier that what makes a reason public is the formal character of reasonableness and that just because a reason is public it is not therefore a good reason. Finally, the debate about the permissibility of abortion shows how even if citizens manage to leave behind their comprehensive views and rely only on public reason, some issues persist and are not resolved. Sometimes, it seems, political values themselves are in conflict and it is entirely unclear which should get priority. For practical purposes we settle these questions through legislation and through the decisions of courts but revisit them. Rawls thinks of public reason sometimes as a way of bringing citizens who are embedded in their different (reasonable) comprehensive doctrines to a point of reconciliation. This reconciliation is not a balance of forces since it rests on political values that receive their justification from citizens' comprehensive doctrines. It is not a way of closing off argument since the political life of a democratic society is always fluid.

Rawls ends his discussions of public reason by considering three main objections. The first objection is that public reason restricts what can be said in public political debate. In one sense this is true. There is a formal constraint on the *aims* of public discourse. However, this is not a restriction on either the content of political debate (that is, on the topics of discussion) or, on the wide view of public reason, a restriction even on the kinds of reasons that may be advanced as long as the proviso is obeyed. Therefore, we can say that the restrictions imposed by public reason are formal and not substantial. The second objection states that the idea of public reason prevents citizens arguing from beliefs that they take to be true. This again is correct but, says Rawls, misses the point of political liberalism and the place of public reason in the theory as a whole. It is precisely because citizens in a democratic society subscribe to differing and ultimately incompatible truths and because they recognize and acknowledge this fact that public political discourse is based on the reasonable rather than the true. We will look at a similar objection to the entire project of political liberalism later. For now we can say that this argument, as it stands, simply asserts rather than argues that truth instead of reasonableness ought to be the standard in public political discourse. The third and final objection resists Rawls's bifurcation between the comprehensive view and the political view that public reason relies on. It claims that public reasoning requires that we hold a schizophrenic view of ourselves. However, Rawls points out that in public political discourse we do not say anything we believe to be untrue from the perspective of our comprehensive doctrine. Indeed, our political utterances are grounded and justified by our comprehensive beliefs. Thus, for example, a political belief in freedom might be embedded in a religious doctrine or a secular conviction. When I forebear asserting the truth of my religious or secular beliefs I do not consider my political utterances false, rather I seek a reasonable agreement with my fellow citizens while maintaining my comprehensive doctrines and convictions. The difference is in attitude and aim and thus not one of asserting the truth in one area of life and what is false in another.

3. The Right and the Good Revisited: Stability for the Right Reasons

We have come to the end of our exposition and interpretation of Rawls's theory of political liberalism. We now need to put it together by looking at how political liberalism answers the question that led him to this theory in first place. His question was: (PL: 4): "how is it possible for there to exist over time a just and stable society of free and equal citizens, who remain profoundly divided by reasonable religious, philosophical and moral doctrines?" Readers will recall that Rawls was led to this question because of his dissatisfaction with his argument in *A Theory of Justice* about how the right and the good intersect. The problem was to connect a conception of justice (what is right) with citizens' conceptions of the good (and consequently their motivation for abiding by what is right, for the right reasons). As we have seen, he purchased stability and social unity in *A Theory of Justice* at the cost of undermining the democratic basis of society; either we have to suppose that all will settle on and agree to the same substantive liberal conception of the good and deny the "fact of pluralism" or we accept democratic pluralism and deny any grounds for agreement on shared political understanding to govern the basic institutions of society. However, now Rawls believes himself to be in a position to escape this dilemma. We can have both a shared political understanding *and* we can accept a multiplicity of conceptions of the good (reasonable comprehensive doctrines). In other words, it is possible to achieve social unity and stability through an articulation of a shared understanding of justice which citizens are appropriately motivated to act on. The problem of stability is thus solved and the right and the good intersect.

To explain stability for the right reasons requires a summary of the preceding arguments. We can begin by saying once again what counts as stability for the *wrong* reasons. Social unity achieved either strategically or through coercion is unacceptable to Rawls. First, a strategic unity is a mere balance of power where citizens agree to a political arrangement only insofar as they perceive that their interests are being served. It fails the test of stability because there is no moral foundation to their agreement and consequently citizens are motivated to keep the agreement only for as long as their interests are being served. A *modus vivendi* agreement of this type is a case of the rational subordinating the reasonable. Second, a unity achieved through the imposition on all citizens of a single comprehensive doctrine can only be achieved through coercive measures by the state. Understandably, this is unacceptable in a democratic society and to democratic citizens. Again, the motivation to abide by the principles that "distribute the benefits and burdens of social cooperation" is of the wrong sort. What the successful coercive imposition of single comprehensive doctrine does is to adjust the pay-offs for actions and beliefs so that it becomes rational for citizens to obey rather than disobey. Aside from the practical difficulty of maintaining such a coercive regime, the point here is that again what motivates citizens is a merely rational concern to protect their interests rather than a reasonable desire to reach and maintain a genuine agreement with others on moral rather than instrumental grounds.

Therefore, stability for the *right* reasons will subordinate the rational to the reasonable and explain how citizens come to be motivated to abide by the principles that govern the basic structure of society. Democratic stability is achieved when three elements are in place. Unsurprisingly, these three elements are those we identified in our discussion of justification in political liberalism. Stability and social unity require that the political conception that governs democratic society be justified in the right way, that citizens take it to be justified for the right reasons, and that the actions of the state in accordance with the constitution are justifiable to citizens. Therefore, what is required is a reasonable political conception (of which justice as fairness is an example) that citizens embrace because the ideas of freedom and equality (among others) in that conception are the central part of their own comprehensive doctrine and conception of the good. Since their own good is at stake we have an account of why citizens are motivated to abide by the principles set out in the political conception. These political values are mirrored in citizens' comprehensive doctrines and are moral values and so the motivation here is moral rather than merely rational. Finally, social unity in a pluralistic democratic society needs an account of how decisions are made and how disagreement is to be handled. The idea of public reason provides a discursive framework that addresses these requirements and thus constructs an account of democratic legitimacy. The decisions and actions of the state are legitimate to citizens, even when some of them disagree, if these are justified by the use of public reasons connected appropriately to the shared political conception. Thus citizens accept the framework for the making of decisions even if they disagree with the particular decisions made by officeholders. Rawls says that social unity is explained in the following way (PL: 391):

a. The basic structure of society is effectively regulated by the most reasonable political conception of justice.

b. This political conception of justice is endorsed by an overlapping consensus comprised of all the reasonable comprehensive doctrines in society and these are in an enduring majority with respect to those rejecting that conception.

c. Public political discussions, when constitutional essentials and matters of basic justice are at stake, are always (or nearly always) reasonably decidable on the basis of the reasons specified by the most reasonable political conception of justice, or by a family of such conceptions.

This is Rawls's answer to the question posed at the beginning of this section, a question that represents the great conundrum of democratic liberal theory. Each point of this extensive and complex argument is, of course, contestable. Many of Rawls's moves in the argument invite disagreement. For example, is a political conception of justice really representative of the right given that it has no reference outside of a historically constituted society? Is justice not a universal value? Furthermore, is the good of citizens really engaged by the political conception? Do they really agree on political fundamentals if their reasons for endorsing these are so different from one another? In other words, does it make sense to say that we share the *same* values when our reasons for supporting them are so *different*? These and many other criticisms will be examined in the following section.

4. Objections and Responses

Political liberalism is a highly controversial theory of justice. This is what makes it both philosophically interesting and worth our attention. I have arranged the objections we consider in a series of questions that critics have put to Rawls. These questions concern the place of truth in political theory, the requirements of justification for a theory of justice, the role of public reason, and the nature of politics in a Rawlsian society. As before, I will set out the objections first and after I have done so I will offer responses to the objections.

Do We Need Truth in Politics After All?

As we have seen, Rawls says that the concept of truth attaches to judgments citizens make in the comprehensive mode. It is there that they assert the truth of their moral, religious, and metaphysical beliefs. In the political mode they abstain from such assertions and instead claim that their political judgments are reasonable, that is, are judgments that others have reason to accept, or, at least, not reject. Therefore, a political conception of justice is neither true nor false and so it follows that justice as fairness is itself not asserted as true.

We have examined in some detail Rawls's motivations for this move, not least of which is the attempt to ground a shared conception of justice in a pluralistic democratic society where there is a necessary range of inevitable disagreement concerning the good.

Rawls's solution is to separate the theoretical concern with truth from a practical concern with justice. I want to look at two arguments that suggest that this approach fails and that, after all, justice does require truth.

First, it can be argued that the mere fact of agreement between people is insufficient to justify the exercise of coercive power by the state over citizens. Remember that the authority to exercise power by the state must meet some standard of legitimacy. The question then is whether the fact of agreement is sufficiently strong enough as a criterion to justify the state in coercing its citizens. The argument against Rawls is that agreement is too weak and that only the claim to the truth is a sufficiently strong enough criterion. We should distinguish between two targets of coercion—reasonable citizens and unreasonable citizens. Now, in some ways the former group has least to complain about since they are part of the overlapping consensus of reasonable comprehensive doctrines; they agree to the constitutional essentials and "matters of basic justice." But this does not prevent them from being coerced by the state because they may have reason to disagree about how those principles and matters are interpreted and applied. However, even reasonable people might wonder, when something important is at stake, whether the fact of agreement, their own included, is sufficient to warrant the use of force against them. Would it not be better if they understood that they were being coerced in the name of a "true" conception of justice? Unreasonable people have more reason to complain since not only is the conception of justice not claimed to be true but they are also not part of any agreement that supports it. They might wonder whether the coercion to which they are subject could have *any* claim to legitimacy if those who exercise it do not ground it in a claim to the truth. Furthermore, since unreasonable people just are those who think that truth should be the criterion of legitimacy they will feel that others are acting from a conception that is not only false but also one that lacks even the proper criterion for legitimacy, namely, a claim to truth. The general point is that where citizens' freedom is concerned only judgments anchored in the truth have the right sort of weight to justify coercion.

Second, it has been claimed that Rawls's argument for a political conception of justice is hopelessly circular. In effect (and very roughly) Rawls argues that coercion is legitimate if reasonable people agree that it is so, and this principle itself is valid because reasonable people agree that it is so. David Estlund who, among others, makes this argument says that "normative political theory cannot hover like a blimp over the moral truth without any point of contact" (1998: 253). We already know that Rawls rejects the idea that there exists a realm of moral truths to which valid claims about justice are beholden. Our justice claims need not correspond to mind-independent moral facts. However, Rawls also rejects, in his later writings, the idea that the content of an agreement on justice between ideally rational and reasonable citizens *constitutes* the truth of the principles agreed to. One possible problem that Estlund develops is that there is nothing special about the agreement of reasonable people over the agreement of any other group. If challenged, reasonable people can only say that their justice claims are valid because they are agreed to by reasonable people but any other group can make a similar claim. Thus, Group X can likewise claim that their claims are valid because the members of Group X agree to such claims (or the basis of such claims). Group Y and Group Z can make the same argument, and so on. The claims have no prescriptive grip on anyone outside the designated group, hence the claim of circularity. Now one would expect a theory of justice to have some prescriptive pull even on those who are not members of an insular designated group. But the circularity of the argument cannot be broken unless there is something beyond and outside the reasonable to which reasonable people can appeal and thereby defeat the rival claims of other groups. For Estlund this "something" is the truth of the claim that what reasonable people agree to (under all the appropriate conditions) validates and justifies principles of justice. In other words, there has to be a point of contact between a conception of justice and an anchoring paradigm outside of the reasonable to complete the justification. The idea of truth provides such an anchoring paradigm and so it is a link to the truth that completes the justification of a theory of justice and distinguishes it from its competitors. As Joseph Raz has argued, "There can be no justice without truth" (1990:15).

Stability or Justification?

These questions about the place of truth in politics lead critics to question whether Rawls provides a justification for a theory of justice or whether he is offering a pragmatic account of how social unity and stability can be achieved. Furthermore, they argue that Rawls conflates these two different tasks and mistakes the latter for the former. Jürgen Habermas says (1995: 110):

> I think that Rawls should make a sharper separation between questions of justification and questions of acceptance; he seems to want to purchase the neutrality of his conception of justice at the cost of forsaking its cognitive validity claim.

Ed Wingenbach (1999: 214) makes a similar argument stating:

> By moving to contextual rather than Archimedean foundations, however, stability replaces justice as the primary objective of the theory.

Finally, William Galston (1995: 627) argues that:

> The formal justification of the liberal state—the strategy to dispense with all specific conceptions of the good—cannot succeed. Defenders of the liberal state must either accept the burden of substantive justification or abandon their enterprise altogether.

Although these critics use quite different terms they all target the same point. They contrast mere "acceptance" of principles with the justification of principles. The thought is that while the social unity and stability of a democratic state can be achieved if its citizens all accept and agree to the same rules, this is not the same conceptual claim as saying that the principles are justified since principles can be justified although not accepted and principles can be accepted although not justified. The claim is that stability is not enough *on its own* to guarantee that the principles that achieve stability are right or just. This criticism goes to the root of Rawls's political liberalism. It suggests that only by connecting principles to some particular conception of the good, some "substantive justification," an "Archimedean foundation" or a "cognitive validity claim" can a theory of justice be properly grounded. However, it was precisely an attempt to avoid having to root a theory of justice in a particular conception of the good that motivated Rawls to develop political liberalism as a response to defects in *A Theory of Justice*. If political liberalism denies that "substantive justification" is possible for a democratic society, then political liberalism simply cannot produce the kind of justification these criticisms demand.

Response to the Questions about Truth and Justification

The claim that at least some political judgments need to be true and that principles of justice require a "substantive justification" that goes beyond "acceptance" and the need for social unity are closely related. They both demand some point of cognitive and normative contact outside of an overlapping consensus of reasonable comprehensive doctrines. I think these criticisms miss the novelty and the challenge of Rawls's political liberalism.

First, the argument that legitimacy requires the state act in the name of truth when it coerces citizens and that political liberalism has no place for truth rests on a confusion. Democratic citizens do think that the political values are true from within the perspective of their comprehensive doctrines (except some who have a comprehensive doctrine that rests on a universal skepticism, if this is possible). However, as reasonable citizens, they do not assert these truths at the political level. For Rawls to assert the truth of a proposition is to simultaneously assert a set of reasons that, in the case of political, moral, religious, and metaphysical propositions, are fundamentally controversial. Reasonable citizens acknowledge the "burdens of judgment." Therefore, the claim to truth always invokes some comprehensive doctrine and thereby invites disagreement from those who subscribe to different comprehensive doctrines. From the political perspective coercive power is exercised by the state on the grounds of a reasonable agreement between citizens on the fundamental political values that structure the basic institutions. This is a sufficiently strong criterion from within the political perspective. But no citizen occupies *only* this perspective. When reasonable citizens are coerced by the state they take the principles that justify this action to be true *from within their comprehensive perspective.*

There is therefore a role for truth in determining the legitimacy of the coercive actions of the state. However, for unreasonable citizens this argument for the role of truth is inadequate. They require not only that citizens, for their own reasons, take the principles of justice to be true but that the state itself assert the truth of these values. However, this would mean that the state would have to subscribe to, and require general allegiance to, some *particular* comprehensive doctrine. This contradicts Rawls's argument that a just liberal democracy needs to accommodate a plurality of comprehensive doctrines. The point is that there is a place for truth in political liberalism and in the argument for legitimacy. We avoid confusion on this point by keeping distinct citizens' political and the comprehensive perspectives. It is the mark of the reasonable citizen that she keeps these perspectives apart.

The second argument concerning the place of truth in political liberalism asserts that truth is required to escape a circularity of justification and to specify what is special about reasonable agreements. In response we should distinguish between a structural claim and substantive claim. The idea of the political is agnostic about its content. It merely makes a distinction between two levels—the political and the comprehensive—and details the relations between these levels. At the structural level the political values shared by a set of comprehensive doctrines could be anything. They could be values that democratic citizens find offensive. Therefore, it is true that, at the structural level, there is nothing special about reasonable agreements. An overlapping consensus between nonliberal comprehensive doctrines would produce a set of political values that would be, let us say, reasonable* for the citizens of that polity, but not reasonable for us. If we confine ourselves to the political level then there is no difference between being reasonable and being reasonable*. However, once we specify the content of particular set of comprehensive doctrines then there is a difference. The political values of reasonable people, the citizens of liberal democracy, are historically and culturally embedded in their comprehensive doctrines. This matters to such citizens and, furthermore, from within their comprehensive doctrines they are sincerely committed to the truth of the reasons that support these values. Therefore, the particular substantive political values that fill in the content of the idea of the political are significant for cultural and historical reasons because they are supported by the comprehensive doctrines of reasonable citizens. It is true that reasonable* people will not be persuaded that liberal democratic political values ought to govern the basic institutions of their society. This is because they have a different history and because they have different comprehensive beliefs. However, it is not clear to me how asserting the truth of "our" political values against "theirs" makes a difference, given Rawls's argument for the burdens of judgment. If there are no ways to settle disagreements about which conception of justice is true then simply saying that one's conception is true takes us no further. From the political standpoint there is a relativistic element in Rawls's argument that some will be uncomfortable with. However, once again, each citizen also occupies a comprehensive perspective where they are free to assert universal truth claims. We are diffident at the political level and assertive at the comprehensive level.

Finally, we turn to the argument that Rawls has purchased stability at the expense of justice. Rawls rejects the dichotomy that the criticism sets up. The argument supposes that there are only two possibilities: either a true, universal theory of justice or a merely strategic agreement that secures stability and social unity. Rawls rejects both of these options by denying that a just democratic society can subscribe to a single true, universal theory of justice and by denying that a *modus vivendi* agreement is enough for justice. As we have seen, Rawls's argument has three moments: first, a political conception of justice which is, second, embedded and normatively secured in a set of comprehensive doctrines and, third, the idea of an overlapping consensus of these doctrines. A political conception alone (even if it is claimed to be true) is not enough for justice since, at minimum, justice requires the allegiance of citizens (the good has to intersect with the right). An overlapping consensus between comprehensive doctrines is also not enough for justice since this would be a mere *modus vivendi* agreement of strategic interests. However, it is the middle element that does the required philosophical work. It provides the reasons that support the political conception (albeit different reasons for citizens who subscribe to different comprehensive doctrines) and it provides the normative dimension that changes mere stability into "stability for the right reasons." It is these three moments taken together that Rawls argues is a sufficient foundation for justice in a democratic society. Insofar as these critics try to impose a dichotomy on political liberalism they misunderstand Rawls's account of justice. It is open to critics to argue that this maneuver fails. Most likely they would argue that here the normative support offered by the overlapping consensus is insufficient to ground and justify a genuine conception of justice. The problem, they might argue, is not whether citizens *can* support a conception of justice from within their particular normative framework but whether they *ought* to. This question can only be settled by revealing a true theory of justice that is justified independently of any particular comprehensive doctrine. However, this latter claim merely asserts what Rawls denies the possibility of. If we are sympathetic to Rawls's claims concerning the "fact of pluralism" and the argument from the burdens of judgment then we too will deny it. Then it would seem we are left either with a general skepticism concerning justice or an alternative such as Rawls provides.

What Kind of Politics Does the Political Allow?

Some critics worry that Rawls's conception of the political excludes and fails to recognize an essential element of conflict and antagonism. These critics argue that political ideas and political practice are essentially contested and that either Rawls is hopelessly utopian in thinking that some political ideas can be uncontested or he is proposing a coercive regime that forbids real political disagreement that is, ultimately, neither liberal nor democratic. Roberto Alejandro (1996: 12) writes that:

> This is an unmistakable trait of Rawls's philosophy: his philosophical method always abolishes tensions by placing them *outside the sphere of deliberation*. The end result betrays Rawls's conception of pluralism and the parties end up displaying a disturbing sameness. The parties in the original position are *one* person, and the same holds true of the citizens of his 'overlapping consensus.' Since they are defined by 'intuitive ideas' which are 'settled convictions' everyone agrees upon, the citizens are also uniform embodiments of these ideas and convictions. They are not plural; they are the same.

Making the point more generally Chantel Mouffe writes (2000: 30):

> Why doesn't his conception of democracy leave any space for the agonistic confrontation among contested interpretations of the shared liberal-democratic principles? The answer lies, I believe, in his flawed conception of politics, which is reduced to a mere activity of allocating among competing interests susceptible to a rational solution. This is why he thinks that political conflicts can be eliminated thanks to a conception of justice that appeals to individuals' idea of rational advantage within the constraints established by the reasonable.

An agonistic view of politics argues that conflict between citizens is an essential part of democratic practice. Conflict, even over the most fundamental values, not only cannot be avoided, it is definitional of an ideal of active citizenship. Critics of Rawls agree that pluralism is a fact about democratic societies but instead of looking for ways to end conflict they look instead for ways to enable it while yet maintaining social unity. This is an important difference. Rawls, it is claimed, assumes that social unity requires an absence of conflict, whereas the advocates of an agonistic politics argue that social unity can be maintained even in the absence of agreement on foundational political values. Mouffe, for example, argues for a distinction between "adversaries" and "enemies" and supposes that citizens are political adversaries rather than enemies who seek to impose their values though without seeking to "destroy" their fellow citizens. Adversaries can live together in a single society and can achieve social unity, although, of course, enemies cannot. Mouffe argues further that Rawls's wish to suppress conflict is dangerous, saying, "It does come back with a vengeance" (31). Rawls does not think that ordinary political activity is free of conflict, quite the opposite. He expects significant disagreement over the interpretation and application of the "constitutional essentials and matters of basic justice." However, these critics are correct that he does connect the possibility of stability and social unity to the idea of an agreement on the foundational principles that govern the basic institutions of a democratic society.

Another way of getting at the same point is to focus on an assumption that informs all of Rawls's writings on domestic justice. This is the assumption that societies are "closed." Earlier we remarked that this was a simplifying assumption that ensured that the contractors in the original position understood that they were making inescapable choices (for themselves and their descendants) and that they would share the fate of their fellow citizens once the veil of ignorance is lifted. Onora O'Neill (1998) has argued that this assumption also *presupposes* "a common political identity" among citizens; arguing that their membership of a particular society, with its history, traditions, and values, is a given for Rawls. As she writes (420): "Yet it is well known that in real life people are often unsure about their sense(s) of political identity, that they may find that those with whom they live in closed societies are not identical with those they regard as their own people, and that not all societies are closed." The point she is making is the claim that Rawls's theoretical assumption of a closed society imposes a common identity on citizens that is at odds with how matters stand in actual democratic societies. Given a common identity it is easier to imagine an agreement between citizens on fundamental political values between citizens and thus to imagine a society in which conflict over such values is absent or minimized. If the assumption of a common political identity misrepresents the meaning of democracy in an important way and the theoretical assumption of a closed society leads to this misrepresentation, then conflict cannot be avoided even on the basic principles of justice. There are obvious implications for Rawls's arguments on stability and social unity. If the absence of conflict is a prerequisite for social unity and conflict is endemic to democracy, then social unity is either not possible for democracy or we need a different argument for social unity that is compatible with an agonistic view of politics.

Underlying these criticisms of political liberalism is the idea that Rawls's notion of pluralism is too weak. He allows for a "reasonable pluralism" of comprehensive doctrines but the diversity of conceptions of the good is much greater than Rawls thinks and if conflict between citizens on basic political values is unavoidable, then the range of reasonable comprehensive citizens will be relatively narrow. Rawls does argue that a just society requires that a political conception of justice is supported by a majority of citizens and that this support endures over a significant period of time. However, as Wingenbach (1999) has argued for example, the idea of the reasonable is a designation that warrants the exclusion of the "unreasonable" and requires the use of coercion to maintain the line between the reasonable and the unreasonable. In fact, some have argued that a Rawlsian democracy would require extensive coercion by the state to prevent "unreasonable" citizens disrupting the political consensus between reasonable citizens. We should be wary of an ideal of a just democracy that seems to require extensive policing of some portion of society designated "unreasonable." We also should be wary of a vision of democratic politics that excludes citizens from the public sphere. These criticisms gain extra traction if we agree that conflict is inevitable in a democracy and if we think conflict is also a desirable feature of a democratic politics.

How Public Is Public Reason?

A final set of closely related criticisms we examine concerns Rawls's idea of public reason. There are two criticisms worth attention. The first argues that Rawls's account of public reason is too restricted in scope and the second argues it is too restricted in content.

On the topic of the first criticism she offered above, Onora O'Neill (1998) claims that political liberalism constructs a limited and restricted "public" that restricts those who can offer acceptable reasons to only those who share the particular attributes of liberal democratic citizenship. She says (422): "public reasoning as Rawls construes it is citizens', hence insiders', reasoning, so may not convince foreigners or outsiders—or citizens who stand back from the way things are, and ask whether they should be that way." Thus O'Neill, writing from a Kantian perspective, challenges the way Rawls limits the scope of the public. The scope is limited in two ways. First, the people to whom public reasons are addressed are specified in advance. Second, what counts as a valid reason is defined as that which is acceptable to this limited class of people. From a Kantian point of view however this kind of reasoning cannot count as public since for Kant *all* persons ideally share the capacities required to offer and accept reasons. It is the presence of these capacities that define our humanity and so it is the metaphysical fact of a universal set of characteristics shared by all persons that makes public reason genuinely public. Once we restrict the scope of the public in the way Rawls does then we lose the normative power of the idea of a public reason. O'Neill's characterization of citizens' reasoning as "insider" reasoning strengthens this argument. Insiders set their own standards of validity by determining what weight reasons are to have in their deliberations. For example, the leaders of a Christian church will likely give more weight to a favored interpretation of the Bible than to an article in a scientific journal when considering their stance on the question of abortion. For someone who is an outsider this weighting of reasons has no claim on her assent. However, from a Kantian perspective public reasons should be such that they have a claim on *anyone's* assent (as long as they possess the minimum capacities that characterize our shared humanity). For Kant the public is *all* and not *some*. Furthermore, O'Neill points out that in cases where citizens choose to adopt a view outside the particularities of their citizenship and of democratic society their reasoning will be deemed nonpublic even though their reasoning has a wider scope. For Kant, the wider the scope of reasoning the more public it is while for Rawls it seems that a wider scope of reasoning may in fact, ironically, disqualify it as public.

The second criticism against Rawls's idea of public reason is an argument directed against the types of reasons that Rawls permits as public reasons. James Bohman (1995), for example, claims that Rawls's "singular" conception of public reason is an inadequate notion of democratic deliberation for modern multicultural societies. Such a notion implies a single point of view within a society that all can adopt. While this is not, of course, a "view from nowhere" in a metaphysical, nonpolitical sense, the idea of a singular public reason assumes a level of agreement about what counts as a reason that Bohman finds implausible. Instead, he says, that political liberalism "needs to assume that 'public' and not merely 'non-public' reasons may conflict deeply as well" (259). In other words, disagreement between citizens on what is properly a public reason is not necessarily evidence of a leakage of the comprehensive into the political but is endemic to public reason itself. Moreover, for Bohman this is not something to be regretted but a way in which citizens, particularly those who are members of cultural minorities, can challenge and assert themselves against majorities. Clearly, Bohman means that Rawls's singular view of public reason shuts out the voices of minorities from public deliberation by imposing an ideal of unanimity on what should be not a singular but a plural understanding of public reasoning.

Response to Questions about Political Disagreement and Public Reason

The agonistic criticism of political liberalism needs careful interpretation. We have already seen that Rawls does not think that a just democratic society will be without conflict and disagreement. The issue between Rawls and his critics is not whether there is conflict or not but rather there is a difference of opinion over what citizens are in conflict *about*. For Rawls conflict cannot go all the way down to the fundamental political values without causing an absence of legitimacy and thus instability. Rawls's approach to this problem is to be expected given that he works from within the broad framework of social contract theory; contractarians take the idea of agreement to be the normative foundation of justice. Proponents of an agonistic approach to justice do not, of course, advocate a Hobbesian state of nature in which conflict unlimited. Mouffe's distinction between adversaries and enemies is an acknowledgment that conflict, even for her, has to be contained in some way. Thus the difference between Rawls and the agonists is less sharp than we might at first think. Furthermore, if we accept with Rawls the difference between agreement "for the right reasons" and a mere *modus vivendi* agreement then we see that the problem of justice requires not merely the management of conflict. In order to achieve justice we also need a moral dimension which, for Rawls, transforms a mere agreement between subjects into a foundation of justice for democratic citizens. It is this moral dimension, limited in scope to the important political values, that resolves conflict on these values, at least for a time. The agonistic criticism either places the limitations on conflict in a different place than Rawls and thus the difference is not about conflict *as such*, or it eschews the moral dimension to justice and legitimacy. Consequently, it is open to the criticism that it fails the test of justice and collapses into a strategic agreement based on interests.

Similar considerations can be brought to bear on the remaining criticisms. While it is true of course that Rawls does presuppose a closed society in his theory of domestic justice at the theoretical level it is not clear that this assumption distorts his vision of a just society in the way O'Neill thinks. While it is true that the political identity of a society and its citizens is always contested it is open to Rawls to say that some level of self-identification as a member of a particular polity is required for the realization of a just society. Political identity is not an all-or-nothing issue and so the level of citizens' identification will vary across time sometimes, perhaps approaching zero in unjust societies. In societies where there is a great plurality of comprehensive doctrines, where, perhaps, there is a great variety of cultural differences between citizens, there might well be struggles over the meaning of a shared political identity. However, this is only a problem if the disagreement is of such a level that there cannot be agreement on any fundamental political values. In this case there is not an enduring majority in agreement on the moral basis of their society and as such this society is not a candidate for justice. Furthermore, if there are no shared values from which the members of this society can draw there is no prospect of justice for this society. Thus, the question becomes what degree of disagreement about a shared political identity is compatible with the possibility of just or nearly just society. I think Rawls allows for much contestation over political identity providing there is a basis in a shared set of values for an overlapping consensus to emerge in time. We are not confronted with a choice between either a closed society with a set and agreed-to political identity among all citizens or a radical plurality of incompatible identities all contesting the collective identity. The real question is what degree of contestation and disagreement on the meaning of a shared political identity is possible for a society that is just or nearly just. I think Rawls in fact allows for a significant degree of disagreement within his framework of political liberalism.

We can now turn to the final set of criticisms. First, to address O'Neill's Kantian criticism. She draws the distinction between public reason as a universal form of reason and "insider" reasoning of the kind used in private associations such as churches and universities. She equates Rawls's account of "public" reasoning with the latter, taking it to be an example of nonpublic, associational reasoning. She does so because the scope of the validity of citizens' reasoning is restricted to the members of a particular society. However, if we recall that Rawls looks for a third moment in his understanding of the major concepts that inform political liberalism we will see that he has a more sophisticated understanding of public reason than O'Neill allows. Whereas O'Neill tries to impose a dichotomy between Kantian universalism and private reasons, Rawls distinguishes among Kantian universalism, private associational reasons, and a third moment between these which he understands as public political reasoning particular to an individual society. Therefore, while Rawls rejects the possibility of Kantian universal public reason for democratic societies, given the fact of pluralism, he resists reducing all reasoning to private reasoning and carves out a space that is both public but not universal. In other words, he resists the pull of the metaphysical without succumbing to subjectivism. O'Neill does not recognize this maneuver and so tries to impose a dichotomy where Rawls is doing something quite different. Once we move from the disjunctive understanding of the idea of the public private distinction a new conceptual space is opened that Rawls exploits in political liberalism. The criticism misses its target because it fails to see this new conceptual possibility. Of course, one might want to argue that there is no third moment but this is not O'Neill's criticism.

Bohman's criticism is directed once again towards the ideal of unanimity and agreement that Rawls seems to presuppose in a just society. His complaint against Rawls is the unanimity that is implied by the idea of public reason and he proposes a plural rather than a singular public reason. It is clear why Rawls would reject this idea. A plurality of public reasons would undermine the possibility of agreement and the overlapping consensus that is necessary for a just liberal democratic society. It would in fact destroy the basis for the possibility of justice since there would be no normative foundation to secure an overlapping consensus and an agreement "for the right reasons"; a plurality of public reasons is just a plurality of reasons and therefore not public in Rawls's sense. He would regard any agreement reached by people who made use of different "public" reasons as a strategic, *modus vivendi* agreement. While Bohman tries to argue for compromise agreements that have a moral content and are not just strategic, Rawls would regard such agreements as either calling on a shared political understanding, thus giving them a normative content, or as having no moral basis at all. He would think that a "moral compromise" was either a disguised overlapping consensus or a disguised *modus vivendi* agreement. There must be some limit to the degree of plurality in a society if it is achieve justice and it seems to me that the very idea of a plurality of public reasons destroys the notion of a public that is essential to the realization of a just democratic society. If we follow Rawls's arguments closely we see that his account of public reason, in contrast to Kant's, allows for a considerable plurality of comprehensive doctrines. It is unclear what is to be gained by fracturing and splitting the idea of public reason further.

For Futher Reading on *Political Liberalism*

Alejandro, R. 1996. What is Political about Rawls's Political Liberalism? *Journal of Politics* 58 (1): 1–24.

Boettcher, J. W. 2004. What Is Reasonableness? *Philosophy and Social Criticism* 30: 597–621.

Bohman, J. F. 1995. Public Reason and Cultural Pluralism: Political Liberalism and the Problem of Moral Conflict. *Political Theory: An International Journal of Political Philosophy* 23: 253–79.

Dreban, B. 2003. On Rawls and Political Liberalism. In *The Cambridge Companion to Rawls*, ed. F. Samuel, 316–46. Cambridge: Cambridge University Press.

Estlund, D. M. 1998. The Insularity of the Reasonable: Why Political Liberalism Must Admit the Truth. *Ethics: An International Journal of Social, Political, and Legal Philosophy* 108 (2): 252–75.

Galston, W. A. 1995. Two Concepts of Liberalism. *Ethics: An International Journal of Social, Political, and Legal Philosophy* 105: 516–34.

Gaus, G. F. 1999. Reasonable Pluralism and the Domain of the Political: How the Weaknesses of John Rawls's *Political Liberalism* Can be Overcome by a Justificatory Liberalism. *Inquiry* 42: 259–84.

Habermas, J. 1995. Reconciliation through the Public Use of Reason: Remarks on John Rawls' Political Liberalism. *Journal of Philosophy* 92 (3): 109–31.

Hampton, J. 1989. Should Political Philosophy Be Done without Metaphysics? *Ethics* 99: 791–814.

Hill, T. E. 1994. The Problem of Stability in *Political Liberalism. Pacific Philosophy Quarterly* 75: 332–52.

Kaufman, A. 2006. Rawls's Practical Conception of Justice: Opinion, Tradition and Objectivity in Political Liberalism. *Journal of Moral Philosophy: An International Journal of Moral, Political and Legal Philosophy* 3: 23–43.

Klosko, G. 1997. Political Constructivism in Rawls's Political Liberalism. *American Political Science Review* 91 (3): 635–46.

———. 1993. Rawls's 'Political' Philosophy and American Democracy. *American Political Science Review* 87 (2): 348–59.

Krasnoff, L. 1998. Consensus, Stability and Normativity in Rawls's *Political Liberalism. Journal of Philosophy* 95 (6): 269–92.

Kukathas, C., and Philip, P. 1990. *Rawls: A Theory of Justice and Its Critics.* Stanford: Stanford University Press.

Mandle, J. 1999. The Reasonable in Justice as Fairness. *Canadian Journal of Philosophy* 29: 75–107.

Mouffe, C. 2000. *The Democratic Paradox* New York: Verso.

———. 2005. The Limits of John Rawls's Pluralism. *Politics, Philosophy and Economics* 4: 221–31.

Nagel, T. 2003. Rawls and Liberalism. In *The Cambridge Companion to Rawls*, ed. F. Samuel, 62–85. Cambridge: Cambridge University Press.

O'Neill, O. 1998. Political Liberalism and Public Reason: A Critical Notice of John Rawls, *Political Liberalism. Philosophical Review* 106: 411–28.

Raz, J. 1990. Facing Diversity: The Case of Epistemic Abstinence. *Philosophy and Public Affairs* 19 (1): 3–46.

Richardson, H., and Weithman, P. 1999. *The Philosophy of Rawls: A Collection of Essays.* Vol. 5, *Reasonable Pluralism.* New York: Garland.

Rivera, L. 2006. Pluralism, Imagination, and Estrangement. *Philosophical Papers* 35: 327–65.
Tan, K.-C. 2001. Reasonable Disagreement and Distributive Justice. *Journal of Value Inquiry* 35: 493–507.
Weinstock, D. 1994. The Justification of Political Liberalism. *Pacific Philosophical Quarterly* 75: 165–85.
Wingenbach, E. 1999. Unjust Context: The Priority of Stability in Rawls's Contextualized Theory of Justice. *American Journal of Political Science* 43 (1): 213–32.
Wolin, S. S. 1996. The Liberal/Democratic Divide: On Rawls's *Political Liberalism. Political Theory* 24 (1): 97–119.
Young, I. M. 1995. Rawls's *Political Liberalism. Journal of Political Philosophy* (2): 181–90.

Part Three
The Law of Peoples

Rawls recognized the need to extend the question of justice to include principles of justice between societies in *A Theory of Justice*. However, he did not offer an account of international or global justice until a short article appeared in a journal in the 1990s. A much expanded and revised version of this article appeared as a book in 1999 titled *The Law of Peoples*. Up until this point, Rawls has been concerned to explicate the principles of justice that ought to govern the basic institutions of modern liberal democratic societies. His assumption had been to regard these principles as applying to a "closed society" into which citizens "enter by birth and exit at death." This assumption was necessary to simplify the theory, for example, by not allowing the contractors to consider immigration and exile as part of their deliberations. Further it enabled him to focus on the main problem of justice in a particular society by assuming citizens are tied to the same fate. Rawls does not relax this assumption when he considers the problem of international justice. He continues to argue that the question of domestic justice is best considered by assuming closed rather than open societies. However, he argues that once we have arrived at principles that frame domestic justice we *then* turn to the question of what principles should govern relations between societies.

The exposition of his theory of international justice has four stages. Rawls first asks what principles should govern relations between more or less just liberal democratic peoples. Once this has been established he goes on to inquire what relations of justice are possible between liberal democratic states and what he terms "decent hierarchical societies." These later societies are not just in the liberal sense explained and defended in *Political Liberalism*; however they are reasonable in the limited sense of offering reciprocal relations with other societies and protecting some minimal level of human rights for their citizens. Much more needs to be said about what Rawls means by "decent" of course and we will return to this notion in some detail below. The third stage of exposition is to ask what relations of justice (if any) can obtain between liberal and decent peoples and what he calls "outlaw states." Finally, Rawls turns to the question of distributive justice between societies, that is, between well-resourced societies and what he calls "burdened societies." We will examine Rawls's account in this order of exposition.

1. Ideal Theory—An Analytic of International Justice

Justice between Liberal Peoples

Rawls divides his discussion of international justice into two parts: ideal theory and nonideal theory. The former is an explication of and an argument for a set of principles to govern the relations between liberal democratic societies. The latter, nonideal theory, raises the question of what justice demands from liberal societies with respect to their relations with nonliberal societies, including when war is justified and when liberal societies have an obligation of aid to nonliberal societies. In the examination of Rawls's theory of international justice we will follow our earlier conceptual division of Rawls's theory into an analytic of international justice and the practicum of international justice, beginning with the former.

The conceptual resources required to address the question of justice between liberal societies have already been worked out in *Political Liberalism.* If we confine our attention to relations between liberal societies then we will notice that a parallel structure exists in the relations between reasonable citizens in a liberal democratic society and between liberal democratic societies in the international arena. In *A Theory of Justice* we recall that although all just liberal societies subscribe to the two principles, the way in which these principles are understood and applied will be different according to the needs, circumstances and history of different societies. Thus, although the veil of ignorance is thick enough in the first stage of deliberation in the original position to mask differences between the contractors, it is thin enough in the legislative and later stages for delegates to the constitutional conventions to make different choices of interpretation and application of the two principles. The result is that we would expect that liberal democratic societies will be more or less just but significantly different societies. Therefore, there will be "diversity among liberal peoples" in the same way that there is diversity among reasonable citizens. Peoples will differ in the political values they subscribe to as peoples; they will value different traditions, and they will have different understandings of their prospects and aims as a society. Therefore, we should expect that, as there is pluralism among citizens in liberal societies, so there is pluralism of the same sort among liberal societies themselves.

It follows from this first assumption that the problem of justice between liberal societies will be resolved by use of similar strategies as those employed by Rawls in *Political Liberalism*. More particularly, he will seek a *political* solution to the problem of international justice; that is, he will expect reasonable liberal democratic peoples to seek a consensus on shared values that does not seek to impose the particular values and traditions of one society on another (not that a liberal society has only one set of values—they are, after all, plural societies). Furthermore, given that liberal democratic peoples are reasonable they will resort to public reason, as we have understood it, as their means of arriving at such a consensus. In their deliberations liberal peoples will offer arrangements and seek understandings it would not be reasonable for others to reject. Finally, and crucially, Rawls's theory of international justice seeks stability for the right reasons. The agreement that is the ground for just relations between peoples will not be a *modus vivendi* arrangement; rather it will be a moral agreement that is fair and which peoples will abide by, not merely because they have an interest in doing so, but because it is right to do so by their own values and standards.

In summary, we can see how Rawls places the same conceptual grid over the problem of justice between liberal democratic societies as he developed for the problem of domestic justice. Of course, the principles of international justice that will parallel the two principles will be different and we will have to explicate the reasoning that grounds these principles. However, before we can move on to consider what such principles might be we first have to address an issue that has lurked in the background of our discussion so far.

PEOPLES NOT STATES

In setting out the problem of international justice we have followed Rawls in speaking of peoples (or societies) rather than states. Most readers will think of the problem of global justice as one that exists between nation-states. "How should relations between nations be regulated?" is a typical way to pose to the problem. However, Rawls rejects this formulation of the issue. The rise of the nation-state as the preeminent unit of international relations in Europe in the seventeenth century carried with it a very particular understanding of what such a state was and what its interests and motives were. Speaking generally, we can say that states were typically understood as existing in a Hobbesian state of nature. This means that states were understood as seeking to advance their own interests *exclusively*. It also meant that nation-states were thought to exist in an environment where what was not to their advantage was usually to their disadvantage and such an environment was one of deceit and mistrust. Readers will recall that Hobbes's own solution to the problem of justice was the imposition of a sovereign authority that held exclusive coercive power and which was able to make the cost of not complying with a constitutional agreement greater than the cost of complying with it. In the international environment of nation states no such sovereign authority exists (certainly not one with exclusive coercive power). Thus, given the assumed rational egoism of nation-states, each state understands itself to be in an endless competition for advantage against other states.

It is obvious that if the Hobbesian picture were accurate, then justice, as Rawls understands it, is not possible between states. In the first place, insofar as states pursue their own interests exclusively they meet the requirement of rationality but fail the demand for reasonableness. According to Rawls, the rational pursuit of private interests cannot be the basis for a just agreement, as we have seen in the case of domestic justice. Second, and connected to the first point, in the absence of reasonableness, stability that is a requirement for justice is not possible. So, although states could come to agreement (each measuring the advance of its own interests in so doing) they would have overwhelming incentives to break such agreements when their pursuit of their own significant interests diverged from the terms of agreement. Furthermore, since each state would recognize this dilemma in their own case and its existence for all other states as well, international agreements would be fragile and, most importantly, lack a properly normative foundation. States are understood as exclusively rational actors. Thus, they cannot enter into and keep to agreements *for the right reasons.* This does not mean that for Rawls they do not, or ought not, pursue their own interests. He allows that societies (or peoples as he calls them) are rational actors but, in contrast with nation-states, they are also capable of being reasonable actors.

States understood in the Hobbesian sense pursue what Rawls calls their "autonomous interests" both in their relations with other states and in their internal relations. The very idea of state sovereignty is one that lays claim to the widest possible interpretation of state autonomy. States are not supposed to "interfere" with the internal matters of other states. They are also expected to seek their own advantage in their dealings with each other. Further, autonomous, exclusively rational, states claim a right to wage war to protect their fundamental interests. Thus, based on Rawls's understanding of states it is not surprising that he chooses to reframe the terms of the debate and our vocabulary. Therefore, instead of talk about states Rawls chooses to speak of peoples as the fundamental unit in the problem of international justice. This allows him to avoid the embedded meanings associated with the language of "states" and move the debate onto a different and a more philosophically productive level.

The notion of a people is a normative concept and not a descriptive one; the same is the case for Rawls's notion of the citizen. There are two basic requirements for assigning the term "people" to a group of individuals. First, what unites individuals into a people is a set of "common sympathies." The idea of shared sympathies is taken from Mill. In Rawls's analysis this is a somewhat vague idea. Rawls cannot mean that a people must share a single comprehensive doctrine to count as a people because that would exclude liberal democratic societies from counting as a people. However, there must be something that unites a group of individuals that makes them count as a unit in a theory of international justice. For Rawls what unites individuals are the shared traditions, common history, and cultural affinities that connect them even when they subscribe to very different comprehensive doctrines. The idea of a *political* theory of justice supposes that there is a shared consensus on some values (even if the justification for these values differs across comprehensive doctrines). This common ground emerges from the contingencies of a common history and common cultural traditions, as well as a sense of a shared future and fate. Rawls needs enough unity to mark off and identify a people without imposing a requirement of a single set of shared values which would contradict the arguments of *Political Liberalism.* Thus, the first requirement of a people is unity. The second requirement is that a people has a moral nature. This means that a people is reasonable in the usual Rawlsian sense. Therefore, a people will "offer fair terms of agreement" in their deliberations with other peoples. Furthermore, a people will abide by the (fair) agreements it makes (providing others are generally faithful to it as well). In short, a reasonable people has genuinely reciprocal relations with other societies. A theory of international justice is not possible, for Rawls, unless the parties to an agreement are capable of acting from moral motives. Consequently, peoples must have moral motives if they are to be the basis for such a theory. This explains why Rawls's account is called *The Law of Peoples.* We need to emphasize that presupposing that a people is reasonable does not mean that a people is not rational; a people has interests of its own that it pursues. Rawls argues that when necessary these rational interests are trumped by the call of the reasonable.

Finally, Rawls defines *liberal* peoples since it is for societies of this kind that he will first outline his theory of international justice. A liberal people, like all peoples, is united by common sympathies and has a moral nature. Additionally, a liberal people is governed by a just constitutional democratic government. Rawls does not require that a liberal people subscribe to a set of particular principles of justice or that it has a particular kind of constitution, for instance, that a liberal people's constitution be founded on the two principles. Rawls instead offers the widest possible interpretation of liberal, which encompasses the following two conceptions. First, in a liberal society the people have effective "political and electoral control" (LoP: 24) over the government—the government is not under the sway of private or corporate interests that subvert a liberal people's democratic rights. The government in a liberal democratic society is accountable to the people. Second, the government in a liberal society protects the "fundamental" interests of its people. Such interests will include the sorts of basic rights that allow for the pursuit of different conceptions of the good, as well as the usual political freedoms and political equality essential to a functioning democratic society. It will also include the protection of basic human rights.

In addition to liberal peoples Rawls specifies four other types of society that collectively make up the world's societies and states. Once Rawls has set out and argued for a Law of Peoples for liberal states, he will process to consider whether these other societies and states can be a part of a "Society of Peoples." The matrix below sets out what differentiates these societies.

	JCD	HR	PC	RofD
Liberal Peoples	X	X	X	X
Decent Peoples*	-	X	X	X
Outlaw States	-	-	-	-
Benevolent Absolutisms	-	X	-	-

JCD = Just Constitutional Democracy
HR = Respect for basic Human Rights
PC = Political Consultation
RofD = Right of Dissent

*By "decent peoples" Rawls means "decent consultation hierarchies," which will be explained later. He also leaves open the possibility of decent societies that meet the requirements of being decent in some other, unspecified, way. Thus, strictly speaking there are five types of society and states.

We will conclude the discussion of what Rawls means by "peoples" by touching on an objection to Rawls's overall argument that is a source of enormous controversy in the scholarship on Rawls's theory of international justice. In light of Rawls's earlier work it is reasonable to ask why he does not simply expand the first original position, and model persons globally. This, the cosmopolitan objection, argues that Rawls already has the conceptual resources required for a theory of global justice and does not need a new theory at all. In fact, individuals' membership in a particular society and their being part of a people is an arbitrary fact about them and should be concealed behind a veil of ignorance. The challenge to Rawls is to justify the move from individuals in the case of domestic justice to peoples in the case of international justice and further to show why the latter move does not involve an unacceptable arbitrariness. We will examine this objection in more detail in the section on criticisms and responses later.

REALISTIC UTOPIAS REVISITED

At the beginning of this exposition of Rawls's ideas we framed Rawls's entire work as one founded on the idea of reasonable hope. We explicated this notion through Rawls's argument for regarding political philosophy as oriented towards what he called "realistic utopias." It is not accidental that Rawls sets out the idea of a realistic utopia in *The Law of Peoples*, his last major theoretical work. The reframing of our ideas about the nature of societies that Rawls requires in his shift from talk of states to talk of peoples seems very demanding. While it is plausible to imagine individuals meeting the normative requirements of citizenship and being reasonable in their dealings with others rather than merely rational it will strike some readers as less plausible to imagine societies meeting the normative requirements of a people. However, we should remind ourselves of the nature of Rawls's task as a political philosopher. He seeks an account of justice (in both the domestic and the international case) that articulates laws and principles of cooperation that *could* apply to real individuals and actual societies and which goes on to argue that such principles *should* apply. We take ourselves as we are as individuals and societies and realistically imagine what we might be. We allow our nature with its limitations and deficiencies to anchor our discussion, thereby attending to the facts of our human existence, without closing off the discussion of what creatures like us could or should be. If we are to extend ourselves beyond merely what is and reach for what might be then we have to be utopian in our thoughts. However, if we are to be not merely utopians, we must attend to our creaturely limitations. This is what Rawls understands by a "realistic utopia." The aim of the vision that Rawls sets out allows for the reasonable hope of not only a just society but also a just world.

The Law of Peoples for Liberal Societies

THE SECOND ORIGINAL POSITION

How then are we to specify the principles that govern relations between liberal peoples? In answer to this question Rawls turns to the same device he used in the case of domestic justice, namely, the idea of the original position. The original position is a thought experiment or "mode of representation" that models the characteristics of persons, their circumstances, and their way of reasoning in order to arrive at an agreement that has a prescriptive grip on "you and I, here and now" (LoP: 30). In the first original position the purpose of the thought experiment was to find agreement between free and equal citizens situated behind a veil of ignorance on principles that would regulate the workings of the basic institutions of their society. The result of the deliberations of the contractors was the two principles which formed the basis for a just liberal constitutional regime. The persuasive power of the original position lies primarily in the fact that it places the contractors in a situation of equality and fairness through the device of the veil of ignorance. The second original position shares the same structure as the first with differently described contractors, with a differently specified veil of ignorance, and, of course, with a different subject of agreement, namely, the Law of Peoples. We will proceed to examine these differences in detail.

The Contractors as Representatives

In the first original position the contractors were individuals seeking to advance their own interests behind a veil of ignorance. In the second original position Rawls understands the contractors not as individuals but as *representatives* of liberal peoples. The question before this second set of contractors is how organized liberal peoples should conduct themselves in their relations with one another. Thus, the representatives reflect the collectivity of a people in the deliberations and not themselves as individuals. We should assume that as representatives of a liberal democratic people each representative is under the effective control of her people. Further, we should suppose that each representative seeks to secure the fundamental interests of her people. As with the first original position the representatives are rational in their deliberations, seeking the advantage of their respective societies. At the same time they know that they represent a reasonable people and are negotiating exclusively with other reasonable peoples.

The Second Veil of Ignorance

The function of the second veil of ignorance is the same as the first. It ensures a situation of fairness and equality between the representatives by concealing from them knowledge that would allow them to shape principles and laws to the advantage of their own societies. There are five pieces of knowledge that Rawls suggests should be concealed behind the second veil of ignorance: (1) the size of the territory the contractors represent; (2) the size of their population; (3) the "strength" of their people; (4) the extent of their society's natural resources; and (5) the level of economic development enjoyed by their society. What they do know is that they represent liberal democratic societies and that their own society and the others they negotiate with are also liberal democratic societies. Notice that the representatives are not prevented from knowing their society's comprehensive doctrine. This is because, as liberal peoples, their societies do not have a single sanctioned comprehensive doctrine; liberal societies exist in a state of reasonable pluralism as Rawls defines this in *Political Liberalism*. The argument for what is placed behind the veil of ignorance is quite straightforward. Rawls begins with the assumption that *as peoples* liberal peoples understand themselves as equal with other peoples and deserving of equal respect from other peoples. There is no *a priori* hierarchy that ranks peoples as superior or inferior within the liberal self-understanding. Of course, history, circumstance, fortune, and misfortune shape how a society fares in the world. For example, the extent of natural resources that is found within a territory (itself defined by an arbitrary boundary) are not in any sense deserved. The citizens of a liberal state inherit a level of economic development and are either advantaged by the labors of their ancestors or disadvantaged. Finally, some societies develop cultures, attitudes, and practices that lead to relative advantages over other societies and again these are not deserved by the citizens of a society who happen to be born into it. As with the first original position, what lies behind the veil of ignorance is what a liberal people regard as arbitrary and contingent advantages. They are not relevant to the normative question of what laws should govern relations between liberal peoples. By roping off the arbitrary and contingent features of the circumstances of peoples the veil of ignorance allows the representatives to reason from the correct liberal perspective and to make an agreement that is supported by the right sorts of reasons.

The Eight Principles

Rawls lists the following eight principles as those that the representatives would likely agree to in the second original position (LoP: 37):

1. Peoples are free and independent, and their freedom and independence are to be respected by other peoples.
2. Peoples are to observe treaties and undertakings.
3. Peoples are equal and are parties to the agreements that bind them.
4. Peoples are to observe a duty of non-intervention.
5. Peoples have a right of self-defense but no right to instigate war for reasons other than self-defense.
6. Peoples are to honor human rights.
7. Peoples are to observe certain specified restrictions in the conduct of war.
8. Peoples have a duty to assist other peoples living under unfavorable conditions that prevent their having a just or decent political and social regime.

Rawls says that the list might be incomplete and does not constitute the final, precise formulation and interpretation of the principles. Nevertheless, most of these principles are common in the scholarship on international treaties and have a lengthy history. As we will discuss later, some of the principles are unnecessary when we confine ourselves to an ideal theory of relations between liberal democratic states. They are aimed at anticipating relations between liberal states and nonliberal states. The first and third principles rest on the idea of freedom and equality between peoples. The veil of ignorance ensures that the representatives have no reason to favor one society over others (since they do not know which society they represent). Thus, agreement on an equal standing between peoples is guaranteed. Freedom and independence are likewise guaranteed by the assumption of equality between liberal peoples which is coupled with the idea that liberal peoples respect each other. Thus, liberal peoples are autonomous and equal and are justified in their demand of respect from other peoples. The fourth principle explicitly states a duty of nonintervention and thus underlines the autonomy of liberal peoples. This is the familiar claim of sovereignty in international relations. However, as we will see, the first and the third principles are qualified by later ones which restrict the autonomy and claims to sovereignty of peoples.

Thus, while there is a claim of sovereignty in a people's dealings with other societies and in its dealings with its own citizens, this claim is in no way absolute.

The second principle follows from the assumption that liberal peoples are reasonable. In fact, it merely gives expression to the idea of reasonableness in international relations. Liberal peoples abide by the (fair) agreements they make in just the way we understand that reasonable citizens abide by the agreements they make. The fifth principle asserts the usual right of a people to defend itself against aggression and denies it the right to "instigate war." This second part of the principle is superfluous when applied to liberal peoples. Such peoples "offer fair terms of agreement" to their neighbors and do not pursue strictly rational goals of conquest and self-interest. Again, Rawls is anticipating the principles that will be required to serve an association of liberal and nonliberal peoples. The same sorts of issues apply to the sixth principle since the mark of a liberal people, as Rawls has defined it, is that it is just, or nearly just. A just liberal democratic society would "honor human rights" since these rights would be protected by an effective constitution. Further, such a society would not need an international treaty to specify this requirement. The seventh principle concerns the question of what constitutes the just prosecution of a war, which is part of just war theory. We will look more closely at what Rawls argues when we turn to some practical issues in Rawls's account of international justice. The eighth and final principle once again concerns relations between liberal peoples and nonliberal peoples. In the first stage of agreement the representatives know that they are negotiating with other liberal peoples who enjoy sufficient prosperity to sustain a constitutional democracy. This final principle will demand a lot of attention later since it specifies the obligation of assistance to other peoples and, in the minds of some critics, supports of a very restricted interpretation of international distributive justice.

Rawls does not test these eight principles against alternative candidates but claims that they are "superior to any others" (LoP: 41). However, he does offer a brief argument to suggest why the representatives would not choose a utilitarian alternative. This argument relies on the notion of equality between peoples that is guaranteed by the veil of ignorance. A global calculation of utility distribution would require that some peoples might be required to suffer hardship *just so* another people could benefit (if such a hardship and benefit boosted overall utility or increased average utility). Given a people's sense of equal standing with other peoples and their insistence on equal respect, such sacrifices would be rejected as a requirement of the Law of Peoples. In just the way utilitarianism is rejected in the first original position because (among other reasons) it fails to respect the differences between persons, the representatives of peoples reject utilitarianism because it fails to respect the differences between peoples.

Rawls says that the representatives "select among different formulations or interpretations of the eight principles of the Law of Peoples" (LoP: 40). There is room for considerable controversy over the extent and limitations on sovereignty. However, given the deep assumptions that lie behind the second original position concerning the kinds of peoples represented in it Rawls's principles select the sorts of laws that would, in some form or another, be chosen. We will get a better picture of the plausibility of Rawls's principles once we have moved through the second stage of ideal theory and examined the Law of Peoples as affects relations between liberal peoples and what Rawls call "decent peoples."

The Problem of Stability and the Idea of Democratic Peace

Rawls is concerned to show not only what principles liberal societies will agree to but also to show that the parties to the agreement abide by them *for the right reasons.* As demonstrated in the case of domestic justice, it is essential that the agreement is stable. A stable agreement is one where the parties do not make purely rational calculations on whether to keep to their obligations but are motivated by broadly moral considerations about what they ought to do. Liberal societies are reasonable in their interactions with other societies (providing they too are reasonable or, as we will see later, decent). Their reasonableness normally trumps their rational motives. This allows them to act not only in accord with principles but *from* principle. Thus, the Law of Peoples is an agreement that is more than a *modus vivendi* arrangement that the parties follow *merely* because they believe their interests are best served by it (which is not to say that their interests are not advanced by it). Therefore, Rawls is following the structure of his argument in the case of domestic justice where he insisted that we have to attend not only to what is right or just but also to what motivates citizens to abide by the demands of justice.

In the international case Rawls is placing his account of justice in direct opposition to the realist school of international relations which views relations between states as resting on a "balance of forces" rather than on a normative foundation. As in the domestic case, Rawls relies on a psychological account of "moral learning" to explain how societies come to have allegiance to principles rather than obedience to a narrow sense of rational self-interest. He argues that peoples, like individuals, acquire an allegiance to principles and thus come to be motivated by normative considerations when they recognize the mutual benefits that flow from acting in accord with principles of international justice. Over time peoples, like individuals, are moved by a higher-order interest in being a principled actor; their motivational framework changes.

Rawls calls stability between liberal democratic peoples a state of *democratic peace*. He argues against the realist alternative, saying first, that such a peace is possible because social and political institutions can be changed and improved and thus fashioned so that human needs can be better satisfied. Therefore, we are not the victims of our circumstances. Second, a culture of commerce and trade allows societies to gain through peaceful means what they cannot or will not gain through aggressive means. Rawls quotes Raymond Aron saying this is "peace through satisfaction." Thus, not only are liberal peoples reasonable in their relations with one another, but they recognize that they best achieve the satisfaction of their wants and needs through their participation in an international cooperative scheme.

Rawls says that the argument for democratic peace and against the realist notion that nation states are in a Hobbesian "war of all against all," is further supported by the historical record. Liberal democratic peoples do not go to war with each other. The "absence of war between major established democracies is as close to anything we know to a simple empirical regularity in relations among societies" (LoP*:* 52–53). Societies that are democratic in their basic institutions, that trade with one another and are members of international organizations, do not go to war with another. Thus, the argument for how stability is achieved and democratic peace is achieved rests in part on conceptual claims about the nature of liberal peoples as well as historical claims.

Toleration of Nonliberal Peoples

The second part of ideal theory asks, what should the attitude of liberal peoples be to nonliberal peoples? Rawls does not expect us adopt a "view from nowhere" and ask what justice as such requires. Nonetheless, as in the domestic case, Rawls approaches the problem of justice firmly from within the perspective of the liberal democratic point of view. From this perspective the question arises of what treatment nonliberal peoples deserve from liberal peoples? Nonliberal peoples do not meet the standards of justice liberal peoples prescribe for themselves. However, as we saw earlier there are differences between nonliberal peoples. Thus, the question arises whether liberal peoples have reason to tolerate either none or some nonliberal peoples?

Rawls refers to two issues when he speaks of toleration in this context. First, one people tolerates another if it forebears imposing sanctions in order to make the latter become more just (or less unjust). This presupposes that liberal peoples have the power to impose or forebear imposing punitive sanctions on other peoples. Second, toleration means offering a people recognition and respect. Such recognition implies that a people has rightful claims on liberal societies and that it is capable of fulfilling certain obligations in a community of peoples. Rawls argues that if a nonliberal people meets some basic standard of "political right and justice" and if its government is capable of honoring international law (as specified in the Law of Peoples), then liberal societies should tolerate such nonliberal peoples. Societies that meet these two criteria Rawls calls "decent peoples."

DECENT PEOPLES

Rawls understands decency as a normative idea that stands between reasonableness and unreasonableness. Thus, a decent people is capable of both recognizing competing moral claims and abiding by agreements. The former seems to imply that although a decent people does not accept value pluralism as a liberal people does, it is nevertheless open to hearing different points of view. This is why Rawls specifies that decent societies are *consultative* hierarchies. They have institutional mechanisms that allow differences of political and moral opinion to be expressed and heard. Second, a decent people is trustworthy in its dealings with other peoples insofar as it acknowledges and acts on the obligations it accepts. In other words, decent societies do not act solely from their perceived rational interests but are capable of overriding such interests in favor of meeting their international obligations under a Law of Peoples. Thus decency is a pale version of reasonableness but robust enough to make the case that decent societies should be tolerated by liberal peoples. In contrast, outlaw societies are fully unreasonable both internally with respect to their own citizens and externally with respect to their obligations to other societies. Once we understand how decent societies meet the criteria of decency we will examine how outlaw societies fail the test of reasonableness and therefore decency.

First, from the point of view of their external relations, decent societies do not have aggressive aims. They do not seek to impose by means of war or sanctions their particular conception of the good on other societies. Therefore, they observe the "laws of peace." Not only are decent societies capable of accepting international obligations but they demonstrate their decency by foreswearing aggressive aims. Second, decent societies respect basic human rights, in regard to their internal institutions and the relations between government and citizens. Third, they have citizens who act from a sense of moral obligation rather than coercion. Last, decent societies have a system of law that is "guided by a common good idea of justice" (LoP: 66).

The "basic" human rights Rawls has in mind are rights to life, liberty, conscience, personal property, and "natural justice" (LoP: 65). His interpretation of these is a weak one. For example, the basic right of liberty protects citizens of decent societies from slavery but does not entail robust rights of political participation. These rights are basic in the sense that they are "distinct from the constitutional rights of liberal democratic citizenship" (LoP: 79). Rawls wants these rights to provide a guarantee of a minimum level of protection so that liberal societies are not required to intervene to aid oppressed and endangered citizens of decent societies. Citizens of decent societies are thus not oppressed but are also not fully free. This mirrors the halfway point that the conception of decency occupies between rational self-interest and reasonableness.

A more controversial point is Rawls's claim that basic human rights are not exclusively tied to a liberal comprehensive point of view. If this was the case, then demanding that decent societies honor basic human rights would be to impose liberalism on them and fail to respect their ideological difference. It would be to demand that they become liberal societies. Rawls does not fully support his claim that basic human rights are "not parochial." It is tempting to believe that if such an argument were worked out it would push Rawls further towards a cosmopolitan position on international justice because it would have to invoke essential normative similarities between citizens of different states. On the other hand, from the point of view of liberal societies, it is difficult to see how toleration could be extended to any societies that did not honor some basic level of human rights. The tension within Rawls's liberalism (and liberalism as a whole) between a normative universalism (as apparent in robust theories of universal human rights) and the demand for respect and toleration of differences, is evident.

Citizens of decent societies act from motives of "moral duties and obligations." Here Rawls means to identify once again the normative character of citizenship. Citizens of decent societies act politically from the sense that they *ought* to so act and not because they are explicitly or implicitly coerced to do so. To be a citizen is to be in a moral relationship with the law and one's fellow citizens where one acts from what one takes to be the right reasons. To be forced to act, even to do what is right, is to be a subject rather than a citizen. Thus, although, from the liberal point of view, citizens of decent societies are not fully free and equal, they are nonetheless at least partial agents in their political lives. This leads to the idea that in decent societies the law is "guided by a common good idea of justice" (LoP: 66). The idea of a people, as a collectivity, already implies some commonality of interests. Rawls takes this idea further by insisting that this commonality of interests is institutionalized in the legal system of a decent society.

Rawls fills out the idea of a "common good idea of justice" through the notion of a "decent consultation hierarchy." Decent societies give their citizens some voice in the political process, although a voice that falls well short of the ideal of political equality central to liberal democratic states. Thus the introduction of consultation elevates decent societies above the floor of oppressive regimes while acknowledging that they fail to reach democratic standards. What is important about consultation is that it gives citizens in a decent society the opportunity to influence the process of political decision-making and also an opportunity and freedom to express dissent. Of course, the government and state institutions of decent societies are not under the democratic control of citizens. Thus, having a voice and the chance to disagree may or may not have an influence over what the government decides. However, there is the implication that the rulers and office-bearers in a decent society are genuinely open to the voices of their citizens. Indeed, Rawls says that they should, if called upon, explain their decisions, thereby introducing a pale version of public reason into the definition of decent societies.

The Third Original Position

Rawls argues that the representatives of decent peoples would agree to the eight principles in a third original position. There are two parts to Rawls's argument for this claim. The first establishes that the representatives of decent societies would enter into an original position along with liberal societies, and the second part establishes that they would agree to the eight principles. Decent peoples are not aggressive towards other societies (since this is part of what makes them decent in the first place) and they recognize the benefits of agreements with other peoples who respect them as sovereign (in the limited sense of the Law of Peoples) and equal. Hence, decent societies have reason to enter into agreement with liberal societies and with other decent societies. In other words, they have the capacity to enter into and stick to agreements because they are decent, and they have interests to further and protect because they are rational. Once in the third original position, decent societies could accept all eight principles. Indeed, some of these principles are tailored precisely for decent rather than liberal societies. For example, liberal peoples have no need for an agreement between societies to ensure that they respect human rights since such respect is a definitional part of what it means to be a liberal state. Furthermore, the eight principles are open to different interpretations and so we can imagine that decent societies would interpret them in favor of greater rather than less autonomy and sovereignty. There is after all an "official" comprehensive doctrine embedded in a hierarchical system of government that the rulers have a great interest in maintaining and securing their dominance. Nonetheless, it is clear that decent societies *could* subscribe to an international agreement on principles of international justice in an original position along with liberal societies. It is uncertain that decent societies *would* agree to these principles, rather than amending them to favor their own decent rather than liberal point of view. Rawls's argument is very thin at this point. It seems that decent societies are presented with the eight principles by liberal societies. Thus, in the original position behind the veil of ignorance they either accept or reject these principles rather than bargaining, as equals with the representatives of liberal peoples. Moreover, it is not the case that the veil of ignorance prevents the representatives from knowing whether they belong to a liberal or a decent society. If this was the case then the principles agreed to would favor decent rather than liberal societies. This is because the representatives would want to ensure that, if they were representatives of decent societies, their conception of the good is maximally protected from interference. The worst outcome, from the point of view of the representatives, is to be a representative of a society that is governed by a single comprehensive doctrine but where the belief and practices associated with this doctrine is threatened by external interference. The best outcome is to be the representative of a liberal society where the belief and practices of comprehensive doctrines is secure. Therefore, it could be argued that in such an original position sovereignty would be very much more robust than in Rawls's eight principles.

This discussion reminds us that Rawls's Law of Peoples is constructed entirely from the liberal point of view and leads to the following question: What sorts of nonliberal societies can be tolerated and what are the terms and conditions under which such nonliberal societies can be tolerated? Thus, the third original position is significantly different from the first two insofar as there is a fundamental inequality between the representatives of liberal and decent societies. The latter either accept or reject principles rather than negotiating the principles as equals.

2. The Practicum of International Justice

Nonideal Theory

Liberal democratic societies and decent hierarchical societies are well-ordered. They are governed by a conception of justice and are thus reasonable or decent. There are three main forms of unreasonable or nondecent societies: outlaw states, burdened societies, and benevolent absolutisms. Nonideal theory is concerned with relations between well-ordered peoples and these latter three kinds of societies. Thus, Rawls is concerned with the practical questions that arise in the real world—a world where "reasonably just constitutional democracies" and decent hierarchical societies face the challenges of noncompliance with international law. More specifically, nonideal theory raises and attempts to answer the question of when well-ordered societies are entitled to go to war against outlaw states? What sorts of means should be employed to bring noncompliant states within the Law of Peoples? What duties of assistance do well-ordered peoples have to societies burdened by misfortune? Therefore, for Rawls nonideal theory has two major aims. First, it asks how well-ordered, reasonable, and decent societies should conduct themselves towards societies that stand outside the Law of Peoples. Second, it asks how these latter societies might be brought under the Law of Peoples and made part of a community of societies.

OUTLAW STATES AND THE RIGHT TO WAGE WAR

An outlaw state is one that uses aggressive means to advance its perceived rational interests. Hence, it fails to meet Rawls's criteria for either reasonableness or decency and consequently cannot subscribe to the Law of Peoples. Well-ordered societies have no right to wage war against each other (nor do they have reason to, as we have seen) and they have no right to wage war against outlaw states either. They have a right only to defend themselves against the aggression of others. This is specified in the fifth principle of the Law of Peoples. This right is grounded in three features of well-ordered societies: (1) they are nonaggressive; (2) they honor basic human rights; and (3) their basic institutions are guided by a conception of justice. Therefore, well-ordered societies have a right to defend themselves to protect and secure their citizens' basic human rights. In the case of liberal societies, they have a right to defend their constitutional rights to political equality and their guaranteed liberties. A well-ordered society has a right to defend its justice-preserving institutions. Rawls defines a benevolent absolutism as one in which basic human rights are respected but which has no common-good idea of justice and has no institutional mechanisms for public participation in its political life. This type of society also has a right of self-defense (LoP: 92). This means that a society ruled by despots who, out of benevolence, honored some human rights has the same right of self-defense as well-ordered liberal and decent societies. It could be argued that human rights cannot be genuinely honored if they are gifts from despots to subjects. A right is a claim made by subjects and citizens against political authorities and fellow citizens and not a gift for which one is thankful. This challenges the very idea of a benevolent absolutism genuinely respecting human rights and, consequently, its right of self-defense. Rawls clearly argues that honoring basic human rights is a necessary condition for the right of self-defense. The question is whether it is also a sufficient condition. For Rawls, a society that failed the test of well-orderliness but nonetheless genuinely respected basic human rights has a right to wage war in self-defense. However, we could argue that genuine respect for human rights exists only as a part of the definition of a well-ordered society. Thus, the idea of a benevolent absolutism that honors human rights is incoherent.

BURDENED SOCIETIES AND THE PROBLEM OF DISTRIBUTIVE JUSTICE

The second part of nonideal theory concerns relations between well-ordered liberal and decent peoples and societies that are not well-ordered because they are burdened by "unfavorable conditions." Burdened societies are those that fall outside the society of peoples because their situation prevents their basic institutions from meeting the standards required to be part of a community of peoples. The principal question here is what duties do liberal and decent societies have towards burdened societies?

Rawls defines burdened societies as lacking "political and cultural traditions, human capital and know-how and often material and technological resources needed to be well-ordered" (LoP: 106). The distinction Rawls draws between broadly ideological factors such as culture and tradition on the one hand and material factors such as material resources on the other hand, is essential to his argument. Thus, the reason why a society is burdened is not only caused by a poverty of resources. Hence, the remedy for burdened societies is not only a transfer of resources from rich to poor societies. Indeed, Rawls argues that a society can be burdened even though it has an abundance of material resources. This might be because its cultural and political traditions prevent it from achieving just, nearly-just, or decent basic institutions. Thus, the problem of distributive justice between societies is complicated by the distinction between the ideological and the material. For this reason, the problem is quite different from the question of distributive justice in the domestic case.

In the domestic situation, resources, in the form of primary goods, are distributed according to the difference principle. The difference principle begins with the idea of equality between citizens in their holdings of primary goods. It only allows for inequalities when these are to the advantage of the least well-off representative citizen. If the difference principle were the basis of distributive justice between peoples then we would begin with idea of equality here as well. This would permit inequalities only if the most burdened of societies benefited. Rawls rejects this approach to the problem of distributive justice in the international arena. Instead of the difference principle Rawls opts for an assistance principle. The latter states that well-ordered societies have a duty to assist burdened societies to become well-ordered, that is, to build a basic structure that is liberal or decent. In other words, liberal and decent societies seek to bring outlaw states and burdened societies into the community of peoples. In the case of burdened societies this amounts to a duty to transfer resources to help them achieve this. This is the positive part of the assistance principle. The negative part states that duty to assist burdened societies is limited to what is required to achieve a well-ordered basic structure. Once a society becomes well-ordered there is no longer any duty to transfer resources to it even if it has a significantly lower or unequal share of the world's resources. Thus, a poor country that is well-ordered has no claim of justice against wealthy countries and, correspondingly, wealthy countries have no duty to assist poor but well-ordered countries.

The argument in support of the assistance principle as a principle of international distributive justice, and against the idea of equality that grounds the difference principle rests on two claims. First, Rawls insists that being well-ordered is independent of the level of resources available to a society. Poor societies can be well-ordered and wealthy societies ill-ordered. Therefore, transferring resources to achieve equality between societies (or making the least well-off society better off under an unequal distribution than it would be under and equal distribution) would not contribute to achieving just or decent basic structures in burdened societies. The latter is the aim of the assistance principle. Thus, there is no reason to seek an equal or justified unequal distribution of material resources between societies. Second, resource-poverty is only part of the reason that a society is burdened. As discussed previously, Rawls argues that ideological factors such as culture and political tradition partly explain why a society is burdened. Thus he argues the following view (LoP: 108):

> I believe the cause of the wealth of a people and the form it takes lie in their political culture and in the religious, philosophical, and moral traditions that support the basic structure of their political and social institutions, as well as in the industriousness and cooperative talents of its members, all supported by their political virtues.

Thus, the distribution of resources from wealthy societies to burdened societies can achieve only limited outcomes since a significant part of the problem for burdened societies is ideological and not material. Therefore, an equal or justified unequal distribution of resources would not alone achieve the aim of building just or decent basic structures in burdened societies. Consequently, it is not the appropriate aim of a principle of distributive justice between societies. Rawls argues that the ideological difficulties faced by burdened societies need to be addressed by promoting, for example, a culture of human rights. In summary, significant (perhaps stark) inequalities in resources and wealth between societies is permitted even if they have just or decent institutions. This would be a world in which just and decent societies are stable and in which no further assistance will promote or aid a burdened society to become decent. Then there is no further reason to distribute resources from wealthy to poorer societies.

Rawls offers two "illustrative cases" (LoP: 117–18) in which he claims that redistribution would be "unacceptable." In both cases the societies are assumed just or decent. In the first one Rawls asks us to imagine two peoples one of which chooses industrialization while the other does not. In the second case two societies with equal resources choose different population control measures. This decision results in one society having to distribute its resources among a much greater population, making each citizen less well off than the citizens of the other society. In both instances citizens of one society are made worse off because of political and ideological choices. Here Rawls introduces the idea that peoples assume responsibility when making political and ideological choices that result in their citizens being less well-off than they would otherwise be. He argues that no redistribution is required provided that these choices do not result in a people slipping below the threshold of justice or decency.

Once a society has just, nearly just, or decent basic structure, it has standing in the international community through its membership of the community of peoples and its acceptance of the eight principles in the Law of Peoples. This standing means that it is fairly positioned with respect to other well-ordered societies in the second (or third) original position. It also suggests that the society enjoys the regard and mutual respect of other peoples. A people achieves its place and respect among peoples not through its share of the world's resources but through the character of its basic institutions. Resource redistribution can only help a society become just or decent in a limited way and the principle of assistance recognizes this. Once a society is just or decent there is no further purpose to the redistribution of resources.

3. Objections and Responses

Rawls's theory of international justice is antirealist. It asserts the claim that relations between societies can have a normative foundation and denies the realist's claim that relations between states is always a matter of the pursuit of self-interest. For Rawls, societies can be both rational and reasonable while for the realist states have only rational interests. He offers no knockdown argument against realism in international relations but relies instead on the plausibility of the alternative theory he constructs. In fact, the issue between realists and their opponents comes down to different ontological claims about the nature of societies and states. For Rawls his ontology of peoples includes the capacity to enter into and maintain fair agreements. Ontological disputes of this kind are notoriously difficult to arbitrate and no amount of empirical evidence settles the question either way. Realists deny Rawls's basic approach to the question of international justice. For this reason I am going to focus on critics who accept a normative account of international relations but who nonetheless find fault with Rawls's theory.

Rawls marks out a theoretical territory between two alternative accounts of what global justice requires. Once again Rawls seeks a third moment between a dualistic conception of the philosophical alternatives. On the one hand, cosmopolitan theorists complain that the scope of the Law of Peoples is much too *narrow*. Thus, the question of basic justice should extent beyond the "arbitrary" borders of societies and the peoples who occupy them. On the other hand, cultural relativists argue that the scope of the Law of Peoples is much too *wide*: it pays insufficient respect and recognition to differences among peoples. Furthermore, it is argued that Rawls is ultimately advocating a form of cultural imperialism. We will look at each of these objections in turn.

The Cosmopolitan Argument

I have divided the cosmopolitan objection into three questions that challenge Rawls's account of international justice. First, the cosmopolitan asks: Why not justice for all (the universalism objection)? Second: Should a liberal people tolerate nonliberal practices (the human rights objection)? Finally: Are the limits on redistribution defensible (the distributive justice objection)?

THE UNIVERSALISM OBJECTION

This is the most general criticism of Rawls's project in *The Law of Peoples.* Ironically, it uses many of Rawls's own arguments from *A Theory of Justice* to mount a case against his theory of international justice. The first premise of Rawls's theory of domestic justice is the equal moral standing of all persons. The veil of ignorance in the original position is designed to ensure that this equality is maintained. Hence, the contingencies that affect equal moral standing are set aside when deliberating about the basic principles of justice. It is, thus, individuals who are given normative priority in the domestic case. However, as we have seen, Rawls gives normative priority to peoples in the international case. The reasons for this can be divided into two kinds. Rawls offers a set of pragmatic reasons for favoring peoples over individuals. A people is located within physical borders and cosmopolitan critics argue that geographical borders are arbitrary from the point of view of justice. However, as discussed earlier, Rawls suggests that borders have the practical virtue of engendering patriotic feeling and engendering an attitude of care towards the natural resources and assets of a particular territory. Furthermore, a people located within a territory it calls its own is able to build institutions that *effectively* realize the two principles or, at least, effectively realize the conception of justice suited to the people in question. Underlying these pragmatic considerations is an obvious skepticism about the possibility of individuals being able develop a sense of loyalty to others and to develop an attitude of care towards their surroundings in the absence of a territorially located people. Furthermore, there is a skepticism concerning the effectiveness of institutions that aim to govern globally or regionally rather than within a specified territory.

However, even if one could set aside these pragmatic concerns, Rawls's main principled reason for favoring peoples over individuals is that cultural differences and thus different conceptions of the good are respected. We should recall that Rawls is very keen to avoid the charge that he aims to impose a specific set of liberal political ideals on others. The cosmopolitan critic asks whether it is necessary to elevate the moral importance of peoples above that of individuals to achieve the respect Rawls aims at. The cosmopolitan would argue that requiring institutions globally to honor individuals' civil and political rights and distributing primary goods according to the difference principle achieves all the respect and toleration necessary. The cosmopolitan argument at this point is roughly as follows. In *A Theory of Justice* individuals are given priority and the differences between them in their conceptions of the good is nonetheless respected. If it is possible in the domestic case to give normative priority to individuals and still respect differences in conceptions of the good, what is it about the international case that is so very different? In other words, the mere fact of differences in conceptions of the good is not enough to ground an argument for the priority of peoples over individuals without undermining the argument for the priority of individuals in the domestic case as well. In response it might be argued that what matters is *cultural* difference. But this will not resolve the issue either unless there is a conceptual mismatch between conceptions of the good and cultural differences.

What could such a mismatch amount to without calling on essentialist differences between persons that track cultural membership and underlie the conceptions of the good that individuals hold? This would be a move that leaves some of liberalism's and Rawls's own basic moral commitments far behind. There are no morally relevant essential differences between persons that depend on cultural membership that are independent of their conceptions of the good. A person's cultural beliefs and practices just are part of what makes up her conception of the good. Therefore, it is possible to respect a person's conception of the good (and by extension her cultural beliefs and practices) without elevating the normative status of peoples above individuals.

In this case, it makes good Rawlsian sense to demand that the two principles be applied to all institutions globally and to demand justice (*as fairness*) for all. This, then, is the universalism objection.

THE HUMAN RIGHTS OBJECTION

Human rights are important to Rawls's account of international justice. Human rights mark the boundary between the category of liberal and decent societies and the category of outlaw states. Rawls claims that some set of basic human rights are universal norms that protect individuals and ought to be respected by all peoples. This raises two objections against Rawls. Thus, it might be argued that human rights, basic or otherwise, are a historically specific, culturally bound, invention of Western societies that therefore lack universal validity. Rather, a human rights discourse is precisely what Rawls seeks to avoid, namely, the imposition of a liberal set of values on nonliberal societies. While it is true that Rawls restricts the set of human rights that applies to nonliberal societies to just a basic few, leaving aside rights to free association and rights to political participation, they are nevertheless human rights and therefore, so the objection claims, an imposition on the values and norms of nonliberal societies. It is difficult to see how Rawls can avoid this objection since he admits to the historical specificity of the values that anchor human rights. One could suggest that either human rights are nonuniversal Western norms, in which case they should not be imposed on nonliberal societies, or they have universal validity, in which case they should be imposed *as a whole* on all societies. In other words, the distinction Rawls draws between basic and nonbasic human rights is bogus and this objection can be made from either direction. It can be made from the direction of those wanting to argue for the universal validity of human rights and from the direction of those wanting to protect nonliberal peoples from the imposition of alien norms and values. I refer to this as the cultural relativist objection below.

Cosmopolitans argue that human rights have universal application and reject the idea that decent societies should be exempt from the full range of human rights. In the second objection what troubles cosmopolitans is that decent societies can deny their citizens rights of free expression and association and rights of political participation and yet still comply with Rawls's list of basic human rights. In short, as long as a decent society refrains from the grossest abrogation of a citizen's rights then liberal societies ought to both tolerate and respect such a society. Decent societies have a common-good idea of justice. Therefore, such a society does attend to the interests of at least most of its citizens. However, as critics point out, the idea of the common good is compatible with intolerance towards minorities in decent societies. Indeed, it is compatible with a lack of toleration towards a minority of citizens who have and advocate liberal values. It seems odd then that liberal peoples should tolerate and *respect* societies that do not tolerate their own citizens who profess the liberal value of toleration. Kok-Chor Tan (2006: 85) argues that:

> The problem of tolerating decent peoples is that it lets down dissenting individual members in these nonliberal societies. According to the Law of Peoples, liberal peoples are not just asked to refrain from intervention in these cases; they are not even permitted to take sides in internal disputes for this would be at odds with the ideal of mutual respect and recognition that liberal peoples are to accord decent peoples.

Thus, the cosmopolitan emphasis on the individual conflicts with Rawls's emphasis on peoples. Rawls subordinates the interests of individuals to the norms of a decent people. Hence, given certain minimum requirements we have already canvassed, it does not matter that some individuals in decent societies do not enjoy the full rights enjoyed by liberal citizens. For many cosmopolitans, universal human rights are the articulation and justification of the value of individuals that trump the interests of peoples and societies. Therefore, Rawls's use of human rights merely as a boundary, demarcating types of societies, fails to capture what cosmopolitans think of as important about human rights, namely, the protection they afford to the well-being and dignity of individuals regardless of the society they live in.

THE DISTRIBUTIVE JUSTICE OBJECTION

Rawls's restrictions on redistribution between resource-wealthy and resource-poor societies will be rejected and criticized by cosmopolitans. When Rawls limits redistribution through the assistance principle, which specifies that peoples have a duty to assist other peoples only insofar as this is required for them to achieve just or decent institutions, he once again relies on the ontological and moral standing of peoples. This is a move that cosmopolitans reject. Cosmopolitans argue for a distributive principle that takes individuals and not peoples as possessing moral standing. They argue that what matters from the point of view of justice is the well-being of individuals. Thomas Pogge (1994: 197) contrasts Rawls's approach in the domestic and the international situation and remarks:

> It does not really matter whether one is born in Kansas or in Iowa . . . On the other hand, it matters a great deal whether one is born a Mexican or US citizen, and so we do need to justify to a Mexican why we should be entitled to life prospects that are so much superior to hers merely because we are born on the other side of some line—a difference that, on the face of it, is no less morally arbitrary than differences in sex, in skin color, or in the affluence of one's parents.

At this juncture we can isolate three arguments against Rawls. First, consider an unjust or not-decent society that has very slim prospects of becoming just or decent. This would be the type of society to which wealth redistribution would not in fact contribute to making it just or decent. Therefore, it would not qualify for very much assistance. It would seem that we are abandoning its citizens to their fate. They have lowered life prospects because they live in an unjust society. This lowered level of welfare is invisible from Rawls's perspective since it is not the welfare of citizens that matters on his account.

Second, consider a society that is just or decent but relatively poor (its poverty cannot be so extensive that citizens' capacity for engaging in the political life of their society is compromised). Again, on Rawls's account their lack of resources is not a reason for assistance from wealthier societies. However, access to resources does matter from the perspective of individual citizens. Because, as Rawls reminds us so often, it is the availability of resources in the form of primary goods that enables us to pursue, and sometimes realize, our "rational life plans." From the point of view of citizens in just but relatively poor societies, it is arbitrary that they suffer a limited or diminished capacity to realize their life plans. Further, societies in a globalized world are not isolated. Thus poorer citizens of just societies will trade with the citizens of wealthier societies. This means that they will measure their capacities against the capacities of the more fortunate citizens of just societies. In short, citizens of poorer just societies will question the moral basis of their relative poverty. Charles Beitz (2000: 694) suggests that: "As in the case of human rights, the attempt to justify international distributive requirements in terms of the interests of peoples rather than persons seems to leave ethically significant considerations out of account and to encourage distortions in our perception of the character of international society."

Third and finally, the kinds of arguments that Rawls's advances in support of his claims for limiting redistribution between peoples are precisely the kinds of arguments he rejects when developing a theory of domestic justice. In particular, it must strike a Rawlsian as somewhat ironic that in his account of international justice Rawls rests his argument on the idea of responsibility. This is an argument that a libertarian might forward. It would be grounds for a claim that citizens within a single society should be free from a state that redistributes resources from wealthy to poorer citizens since everyone is responsible for their own condition (in the absence of coercion and fraud). Rawls does not think this is a good argument in the case of domestic justice and so it is worth asking why it should be a good argument when it comes to peoples. Why does responsibility have argumentative leverage here but not in the domestic case?

The Cultural Relativist Argument

The cosmopolitan argument objects to the narrowness of Rawls's theory of international justice. The cultural relativist argument alleges the opposite error. It claims that Rawls's argument is too broad in its reach. Whereas the cosmopolitan argues that individual well-being trumps peoples, the cultural relativist argues that peoples and their cultural autonomy trump concern for (what universalist liberals consider) the well-being of individuals. Rawls's argument against cosmopolitans is based on the primacy he gives to toleration and respect; however, the cultural relativist would argue that toleration and respect demand more than Rawls is willing to give. More specifically, a cultural relativist might argue that the basic human rights Rawls demands as a minimum requirement for a people to qualify as a decent society is an imposition of very particular Western and liberal standards on peoples who do not share the values that anchor these rights. In other words, Rawls is committed to *some* universalism, in short, a universality of basic human rights. Rawls is thus prescribing and imposing values in the way that a cultural relativist argues all liberals do, cosmopolitan or Rawlsian. Catherine Audard (2006: 59–60) summarizes this position: "Because the Law of Peoples advocated by Rawls is an extension of a liberal conception of justice, it cannot escape its origins, and may not be acceptable to non-Western cultures. It is little more in the end, than and expression of cultural imperialism." The fact that Rawls is circumscribed in the extent to which he does impose a human rights requirement is no defense in the eyes of a cultural relativist; any imposition of culturally specific values is objectionable to a cultural relativist.

Response to the Cosmopolitan Argument and the Cultural Relativist Argument

The cosmopolitan criticisms rest on a framework for understanding the requirements of international justice that Rawls rejects. Charles Beitz (2000:677) labels Rawls's framework "social liberalism." Social liberalism takes the question of justice to be an issue for societies to settle themselves, as an internal matter, and the international order to ideally provide the background conditions that enable societies to build and maintain just institutions. *The Law of Peoples* is thus a defense and elaboration of the social liberal approach to the problem of global justice.

The complaints cosmopolitan liberals raise against Rawls are not issues of detail but are directed to his very approach to the issues and so we are asked to decide between frameworks, not merely between arguments. Thus, the universalism objection acquires its purchase and forcefulness *only* if we adopt the cosmopolitan's view. This perspective suggests that obtaining justice for individuals is a matter that goes beyond the concerns of particular societies and their institutions (allowing that breaches of basic human rights are, for Rawls, a legitimate international concern that transcends the sovereignty of particular societies). Much rests on the cogency of Rawls's arguments for the ontological and moral status of peoples. We have already examined this debate in detail and noted the allegation that Rawls's claim is empirically and conceptually weak. However, I think the empirical issues are not settled either way. In fact, there is little or no direct empirical evidence on what effect global basic institutions would have on the well-being and political freedoms of individuals. Thus the cosmopolitan argument while alleging empirical deficiencies in Rawls's claims for the importance of peoples has only speculative empirical claims favoring its own approach. Like Immanuel Kant, Rawls is deeply skeptical of the idea of global government. Thus, while the universalism objection is attractive for its simplicity and its congruence with Rawls's own approach to achieving domestic justice, it is deficient with regard to the practicality of its proposals. Therefore, it is not something we can *reasonably* hope for.

Once we appreciate the fact that Rawls offers an alternative framework we can more easily understand that his approach is anchored in the perspective of the liberal state and not in the cosmopolitan perspective of a universal "Archimedean point." Rawls inquires into the extent and the limits of toleration that liberal states ought to abide by. This is why some have suggested that Rawls offers not a theory of global justice but a guide to foreign policy for liberal states. This is true to some extent but Rawls's theory is grounded in an extensive philosophical argument; it has an importance that goes beyond mere "foreign policy recommendations." This argument rests on a liberal commitment to toleration and respect for the plurality of peoples in the world. Given this grounding commitment there is nothing odd about asking what a liberal people can and will tolerate in the practices of nonliberal peoples. In fact, since justice for individuals is a matter for societies to settle, it is the *only* question that can be asked by the liberal state. Thus, the cosmopolitan complaint that Rawls treats human rights not as a matter of global individual welfare but as a boundary concept dividing the tolerable from the intolerable is correct. Nevertheless, it is one that Rawls would deny is problematic for an argument offered from within the framework of social liberalism. Furthermore, it is not that Rawls is unconcerned that all should enjoy the full catalogue of liberal human rights. Rather he suggests that a liberal people should not impose this liberal catalogue on other peoples. Therefore, if a society meets the requirement of respecting basic human rights (and is nonaggressive, etc.) Rawls argues that a liberal people should respect and tolerate it as it is a decent society although not a liberal one. The distinction between a decent and a liberal society is not one that a cosmopolitan liberal will accept. Thus, the issue is not the scope of human rights, as cosmopolitans allege, but rather one of framework and the commitment to toleration. Part of the problem is that Rawls does not explain what makes some rights basic and others specific to liberal societies. The differences between these two classes of rights might be intuitive (the latter dealing mainly with political freedoms and the former dealing with moral claims) but it is not theoretically grounded in the original position where the contractors do not make a distinction between rights in this way.

The final cosmopolitan objection concerning distributive justice rests on a different global justice framework. If, as Rawls argues, distributive justice can only be achieved within particular societies, then there is nothing to be gained from asking how resources should be distributed globally among individuals. Rawls *does* think that liberal states should redistribute resources to maintain, support, and grow just institutions in societies that are vulnerable to failing and so are "burdened." However, the proper perspective is not the relative well-being of individuals across the globe but, once again, the perspective of the liberal state asking what its obligations are to *other states.* Commentators have pointed out that the obligation to foster the just institutions of poorer burdened liberal and decent societies is not a small obligation at all. It would require much more aid than actual liberal states now offer. In fact, this approach to international aid would most likely require quite considerable redistribution. It is true that individuals in some societies would be worse off, materially, than they would be under an application of the difference principle on a global scale and that this relative poverty is invisible from the social liberal perspective. This only really counts as an objection if distributive justice can be achieved on a global scale. However, Rawls is skeptical that political justice is compatible with the existence of global institutions on a scale large enough to implement a principle like the difference principle. Liberal states *are* concerned that all individuals have their basic human rights respected in whatever society they live in. I would argue, that this in itself might require some redistribution of resources even to people who live in outlaw states (to protect their right to bodily integrity for example). Furthermore, we should also assume that individuals who live in (nearly) just and decent societies but whose states are less well-off than other (nearly) just or decent societies must, nonetheless, be well-off enough to be able to be effective and functioning citizens. In other words, it would be easy to exaggerate how much difference there can be between citizens of societies that are all (nearly) just or decent given the level of resources citizens require to be effective members of their societies. It could be argued, paradoxically, that individual well-being is better served by Rawls's social liberal approach than by the cosmopolitan liberal's alternative.

The cultural relativist's objection that Rawls goes too far in insisting on universal basic human rights and that this is evidence of intolerance and disrespect of other peoples, can only be met by saying that a liberal has to care to some extent about how individuals fare in other societies. It would be an odd liberalism that tolerated *anything*. Hence, the liberal has to draw a line somewhere. Rawls draws his line at the point of basic human rights. It is true that Rawls does not offer much argument for what makes these rights basic. At the same time, they have an intuitive appeal and seem to mark off what a liberal must be committed to if she is to be a liberal at all. The cultural relativist's complaint then is not so much that Rawls goes too far but that Rawls is a liberal; this is a charge Rawls is more than willing to accept.

For Further Reading on *The Law of Peoples*

Audard, C. 2006. Cultural Imperialism and 'Democratic Peace'. In *Rawls's Law of Peoples: A Realistic Utopia?*, ed. R Martin and D. A. Reidy, 59–75. Oxford: Blackwell.

Beitz, C. 2000. Rawls's Law of People. *Ethics* 110: 669–96.

Buchanan, A 2000. Rawls's Law of Peoples: Rules for a Vanished Westphalian World. *Ethics* 110 (4): 697–21.

Caney, S. 2002. Survey Article: Cosmopolitanism and the Law of Peoples. *Journal of Political Philosophy* 10 (1): 95–123.

Hayden, P. 2002. *John Rawls: Towards a Just World Order*. Cardiff: University of Wales Press.

Moellendorf, D. 1996. Constructing a Law of Peoples. *Pacific Philosophical Quarterly* 77 (2): 132–54.

———. 2002. *Cosmopolitan Justice*. Boulder, CO: Westview Press.

Martin, R., and Reidy, D. A. 2006. *Rawls's Law of Peoples: A Realistic Utopia?* Oxford: Blackwell.

Pogge, T. 1994. An Egalitarian Law of Peoples. *Philosophy and Public Affairs* 23 (3): 195–224.

Tan, K. C. 1998. Liberal Toleration in Rawls's Law of Peoples. *Ethics* 108: 276–95.

———. 2006. The Problem of Decent Peoples. In. *Rawls's Law of Peoples: A Realistic Utopia?*, ed. R Martin and D. A. Reidy, 76–94. Oxford: Blackwell.

Conclusion

We live in world that is increasingly unjust. In many liberal democratic societies the gap between the best-off and the worst-off grows larger. Other societies pursue economic growth while remaining blind to their citizens' political rights and freedoms. The citizens of some other societies are so bereft of basic resources that they struggle to maintain their human dignity. Additionally, there is widespread intolerance. Governments of the West seek to export democracy through force and "nonstate actors," as they are called, seek to impose their idea of the good through force and terror.

In this context Rawls challenges us to see the world through the lens of fairness. Once we adjust our vision we see the immense and real injustices people suffer. Sometimes this suffering is as close as a neighbor who lacks basic health security or someone across the world with inadequate access to food and clean water. Sometimes it is not the injustice of poverty but of rights and freedoms denied. In this book I have shown that Rawls throws out more than just a challenge in inviting us to see the world in its stark unfairness. He also lays out a path away from injustice.

Injustice can only be effectively challenged if we can articulate, to ourselves and to others, both why a situation is unjust and how we might move towards justice. Political philosophy at its best offers both an answer to the why of injustice and the how of political and economic change. By this measure no one in the recent history of philosophy has been clearer in stating what makes a situation unjust while offering at the same time a vision of a possible future just world. This is not to say that Rawls is correct in every philosophical argument he offers. I hope this book has shown that he is not. I am persuaded, though, that if we keep our heads above the battles over philosophical details and keep our eyes on Rawls's vision of justice as fairness, we will have sight of a world worth living and fighting for.

I hope that my account of Rawls's ideas and arguments will have moved readers to further explore his philosophical work. Additionally, I hope that readers will have come to appreciate the immense craft of his arguments. Some might even be moved to adopt the Rawlsian vision of justice. If we can understand the world we can change it. To achieve this we do not need the utopian aspirations of fanatics. We can also avoid the opposite vice in the quiet despair of apathetic consumerism, and instead follow Rawls in the *reasonable hope* of a just society in a just world. This is not easy in the present atmosphere of hostility and fear where those who have possession of the treasures of the world seem eager only to acquire more and to turn away from the rights and claims of others. With this bleak vision of the world in mind let us consider a quotation from the political philosopher Martha Nussbaum (2002: 21), which captures the power and promise of Rawls's work and the alternative vision he spent a lifetime arguing for.

> America has increasingly moved away from John Rawls. Inequalities have grown, and the electorate seems largely indifferent to them. But our own greed and partiality can hardly diminish the virtues of his distinguished work. Perhaps we can regard the occasion of his death as a challenge to look into ourselves and identify the roots of those selfish passions that eclipse, so much of the time, the vision of the general good. Purity of heart would be to see clearly what has blocked that vision and to act with grace and self-command toward the general good.

Bibliography

Major Works by Rawls

1971. (Revised 1999) *A Theory of Justice*. Cambridge: Harvard University Press.

1993. *Political Liberalism*. New York: Columbia University Press.

1999. *The Law of Peoples*. Cambridge: Harvard University Press.

1999. *Collected Papers*. Edited by S. Freeman. Cambridge: Harvard University Press.

2000. *Lectures on the History of Moral Philosophy*. Edited by B. Herman. Cambridge: Harvard University Press.

2001. *Justice as Fairness: A Restatement*. Edited by E. Kelly. Cambridge: Harvard University Press.

Criticism and Commentary

Alejandro, R. 1993. Rawls's Communitarianism. *Canadian Journal of Philosophy* 23: 75–99.

———. 1996. What is Political about Rawls's Political Liberalism? *Journal of Politics* 58 (1): 1–24.

Barry, B. 1973. The Liberal Theory of Justice: A Critical Examination of the Principal Doctrines in *A Theory of Justice* by John Rawls. Oxford: Clarendon Press.

———. 1973. John Rawls and the Priority of Liberty. *Philosophy and Public Affairs* 2: 274–90.

———. 1995. John Rawls and the Search for Stability. *Ethics* 105 (4): 874–915.

———. 1998. *The Limits of Rawlsian Justice*, Baltimore: Johns Hopkins Press.

Beauchamp, T. 1980. Distributive Justice and the Difference Principal. In *John Rawls's Theory of Social Justice*, ed. H. Gene Blocker and Elizabeth H. Smith, 132–61. Ohio University Press.

Beitz, C. 1979. *Political Theory and International Relations.* Princeton, NJ: Princeton University Press, 127–69.

———. 2000. Rawls's Law of People. *Ethics* 110: 669–96.

Boettcher, J. W. 2004. What Is Reasonableness? *Philosophy and Social Criticism* 30: 597–621.

Bohman, J. F. 1995. Public Reason and Cultural Pluralism: Political Liberalism and the Problem of Moral Conflict. *Political Theory* 23: 253–79.

Brink, D. 1987. Rawlsian Constructivism in Moral Theory. *Canadian Journal of Philosophy*: 71–90.

Buchanan, A. 1989. Assessing the Communitarian Critique of Liberalism. *Canadian Journal of Philosophy* 23: 75–99.

———. 2000. Rawls's Law of Peoples: Rules for a Vanished Westphalian World. *Ethics* 110 (4): 697–721.

Caney, S. 2001. Cosmopolitanism and the Law of Peoples. *Journal of Political Philosophy* 9 (3): 9979. 1–29.

Clark, B., and Gintis, H. 1978. Rawlsian Justice and Economic Systems. *Philosophy and Public Affairs* 7 (4): 302–25.

Crocker, L. 1977. Equality, Solidarity and Rawls's Maximin. *Philosophy and Public Affairs* 6: 262–66.

Daniels, N. 1975. Equal Liberty and Unequal Worth of Liberty. *Reading Rawls: Critical Studies on Rawls's A Theory of Justice.* New York: Basic Books, 253–81.

———. 1979. Wide Reflective Equilibrium and Theory Acceptance in Ethics. *Journal of Philosophy*, 76: 256–82.

———. 1989. *Reading Rawls.* New York: Basic Books.

———. 1996. *Justice and Justification.* Cambridge: Cambridge University Press, 144–75.

Darwall, S. L. 1976. A Defense of the Kantian Interpretation. *Ethics* 86 (2): 164–70.

Dreban, B. 2003. On Rawls and Political Liberalism. In *The Cambridge Companion to Rawls*, ed. F. Samuel. Cambridge: Cambridge University Press, 316–46.

Dworkin, R. 1973. The Original Position. *University of Chicago Law Review* 40: 500–533.

English, J. 1977. Justice between Generations. *Philosophical Studies* 31: 91–104.

Estlund, D. 1998. The Insularity of the Reasonable: Why Political Liberalism Must Admit the Truth. *Ethics* 108 (2): 252–75.

Galston, W. A. 1989. Pluralism and Social Unity. *Ethics* 99 (4): 711–26.

———. 1995. Two Concepts of Liberalism. *Ethics: An International Journal of Social, Political, and Legal Philosophy* 105: 516–34.

Gaus, G. F. 1999. Reasonable Pluralism and the Domain of the Political: How the Weaknesses of John Rawls's *Political Liberalism* Can be Overcome by a Justificatory Liberalism. *Inquiry* 42: 259–84.

Gauthier, D. 1974. Justice and Natural Endowment: Toward a Critique of Rawls's Ideological Framework. *Social Theory and Practice* 3: 3–26.

Goldman, A. H. 1976. Rawls's Original Position and the Difference Principle. *Journal of Philosophy* 73: 845–49.

Gutmann, A. 1989. The Central Role of Rawls's Theory. *Dissent* 36: 338–42.

Habermas, J. 1995. Reconciliation through the Public Use of Reason: Remarks on John Rawls's Political Liberalism. *Journal of Philosophy* 92: 109–31.

Hampton, J. 1989. Should Political Philosophy Be Done without Metaphysics? *Ethics* 99: 791–814.

Hare, R. M. 1973. Rawls's Theory of Justice. *Philosophical Quarterly* 23: 144–55.

Hart, H. L. A. 1973. Rawls on Justice. *Ethics* 83: 294–307.

Harsanyi, J. 1975. Can the Maximin Principle Serve as a Basis for Morality? A critique of John Rawls's Theory. *American Political Science Review* 69: 594–606.

Held, V. 1976. On Rawls and Self-Interest. *Midwest Studies in Philosophy* 1: 57–60.

Hill, T. E., Jr. 1989. Kantian Constructivism in Ethics. *Ethics* 99: 752–70.

———. 1994. The Problem of Stability in *Political Liberalism. Pacific Philosophy Quarterly* 75: 332–52.

Jackson, M. W. 1985. Aristotle on Rawls: A Critique of Quantitative Justice. *Journal of Value Inquiry* 19: 99–110.

Kai, N. 1977. The Choice Between Perfectionism and Rawlsian Contractarianism. *Interpretation* 6: 132–39.

Kaufman, A. 2006. Rawls's Practical Conceptio–n of Justice: Opinion, Tradition and Objectivity in Political Liberalism. *Journal of Moral Philosophy: An International Journal of Moral, Political and Legal Philosophy* 3: 23–43.

Klosko, G. 1993. Rawls's 'Political' Philosophy and American Democracy. *American Political Science Review* 87 (2): 348–59.

———. Political Constructivism in Rawls's Political Liberalism. *American Political Science Review* 91 (3): 635–46.

Krasnoff, L. 1998. Consensus, Stability and Normativity in Rawls's *Political Liberalism. Journal of Philosophy* 95 (6): 269–92.

Kukathas, C. and Philip, P. 1990. *Rawls: A Theory of Justice and Its Critics.* Stanford: Stanford University Press.

Laden, A. S. 2004. Taking the Distinction between Persons Seriously. *Journal of Moral Philosophy: An International Journal of Moral, Political and Legal Philosophy* 1: 277–92.

Larmore, C. 2001. Lifting the Veil. *The New Republic*, no. 4490: 32–37.

Lyons, D. 1972. Rawls Versus Utilitarianism. *Journal of Philosophy* 69: 535–45.

Mandle, J. 1999. The Reasonable in Justice as Fairness. *Canadian Journal of Philosophy* 29: 75–107.

Miller, R. 1974. Rawls and Marxism. *Philosophy and Public Affairs* 3: 167–91.

Moellendorf, D. 1996. Constructing the Law of Peoples. *Pacific Philosophical Quarterly* 77: 132–54.

Moore, M. 1996. On Reasonableness. *Journal of Applied Philosophy* 13: 167–77.

Mouffe, C. 2000. *The Democratic Paradox*. New York: Verso.

———. 2005. The Limits of John Rawls's Pluralism. *Politics, Philosophy and Economics* 4: 221–31.

Nagel, T. 1973. Rawls on Justice. *Philosophical Review* 82: 220–34.

———. 1999. The Rigorous Compassion of John Rawls. *The New Republic*: 36–41.

———. 2003. Rawls and Liberalism. In *The Cambridge Companion to Rawls*, ed. F. Samuel, 62–85. Cambridge: Cambridge University Press.

Narveson, J. 1982. Rawls and Utilitarianism. In *The Limits of Utilitarianism*, ed. Harlan B. Miller and William H. Williams, 128–42. Minneapolis: University of Minnesota Press.

Nozick, R. 1974. Distributive Justice. In his *Anarchy, State and Utopia*, 149–231. New York: Basic Books.

Nussbaum, M. 2001. The Enduring Significance of John Rawls. *The Chronicle of Higher Education*, July 20, 2001.

———. 2002. Making Philosophy Matter to Politics. *The New York Times*, December 2, 21.

Okin, S. M. 1987. Justice and Gender. *Philosophy and Public Affairs* 16 (1): 42–72.

O'Neill, O. 1998. Political Liberalism and Public Reason: A Critical Notice of John Rawls, Political Liberalism. *Philosophical Review* 106: 411–28.

Pogge, T. 1981. The Kantian Interpretation of Justice as Fairness. *Zeitschrift für philosophische Forschung* 35: 47–65.

———. 1989. *Realizing Rawls*. Ithaca: Cornel University Press.

———. 1994. *John Rawls*. Munich: C.H. Beck.

———. 2007. *John Rawls: His Life and Theory of Justice*. Oxford: Oxford University Press.

Raz, J. 1990. Facing Diversity: The Case of Epistemic Abstinence. *Philosophy and Public Affairs* 19 (1): 3–46.

Richardson, H., and Weithman, P. 1999. *The Philosophy of Rawls: A Collection of Essays*. 5 vols. New York: Garland.

Rivera, L. 2006. Pluralism, Imagination, and Estrangement. *Philosophical Papers* 35: 327–65.

Rogers, B. 1999. Behind the Veil. *Lingua Franca* 9 (5): 57–65.

Sandel, M. J. 1984. The Procedural Republic and the Unencumbered Self. *Political Theory* 12 (1): 81–96.

———. 1994. Political Liberalism. *Harvard Law Review* 107: 1763–794.

———. 1998. *Liberalism and the Limits of Justice*. Cambridge: Cambridge University Press.

Scheffler, S. 1994. The Appeal of Political Liberalism. *Ethics* 105 (1): 4–22.

Sen, A. 2006. What Do We Want from a Theory of Justice? *Journal of Philosophy* 103: 215–38.

Sterba, J. 1974. Justice as Desert. *Social Theory and Practice* 3: 101–16.

Talisse, R. B. 2001. On Rawls: A Liberal Theory of Justice and Justification. Belmont, CA: Wadsworth.

Tan, K. C. 1998. Liberal Toleration in Rawls's Law of Peoples. *Ethics* 108 (2): 276–95.

———. 2001. Reasonable Disagreement and Distributive Justice. *Journal of Value Inquiry* 35: 493–507.

Taylor, R. S. 2003. Rawls's Defense of the Priority of Liberty: A Kantian Reconstruction. *Philosophy and Public Affairs* 31: 246–71.

Waldron, J. 1999. The Plight of the Poor in the Midst of Plenty. *London Review of Books* 21, no. 14: 3–6.

Weinstock, Daniel. 1994. The Justification of Political Liberalism. *Pacific Philosophical Quarterly* 75.

Wingenbach, E. 1999. Unjust Context: The Priority of Stability in Rawls's Contextualized Theory of Justice. *American Journal of Political Science* 43 (1): 213–32.

Wolff, R. P. 1977. *Understanding Rawls*. Princeton, NJ: Princeton University Press.

Wolin, S. S. 1996. The Liberal/Democratic Divide: On Rawls's *Political Liberalism*. *Political Theory* 24 (I): 97–119.

Young, I. M. 1995. Rawls's *Political Liberalism*. *Journal of Political Philosophy* 3 (2): 181–90.

Index

www.ingramcontent.com/pod-product-compliance
Lightning Source LLC
Jackson TN
JSHW021416170426
101040JS00011B/141

* 9 7 8 0 8 1 2 6 9 6 8 0 6 *